"This is one of the best written guides for creating alliance networks, which are needed for success in highly global, complex and competitive markets. It provides not only valuable academic concepts for building and developing networks, but also sound practical ideas on how to jointly develop value with partners. A must read."
Jean-Christophe Visentin, Head of Strategic Alliances, Orange Business Services

"In an increasingly globalized world, companies are faced with a growing number of challenges—new regulations, disruptive technologies and evolving value chains. These are impossible to tackle alone and require learning how to cooperate with others. The tools, anecdotes, cases and lessons from *Network Advantage* would be handy to CEOs and corporate strategists who are looking to make alliances and partnerships a source of competitive advantage for their organizations. This book is a must read."
Yash Khanna, Director, UK & Europe, Tata Consultancy Services

"In today's world, cooperation is an important driver of business success. Yet in the excitement following the announcements of new alliances and partnerships, executives often approach them without a truly strategic view of how they fit with their companies' long-term goals. The not-to-be-missed insights, ideas and tools contained in this book will help all executives to not only ensure that each and every alliance they form has a solid foundation, but also that the entire portfolio of alliances helps their firm to achieve its objectives."
Julie Wrazel, Ph.D., VP Strategic Alliances, Pacific Nanoscience

"Although many executives understand the importance of collaboration, they lack the big picture of how all of their alliances and partnerships fit in a coherent whole. *Network Advantage* does a great job of bridging academic research and practical examples to help companies re-discover their competitive advantage. This is a great guidebook to all senior executives."
Marie-Noëlle Castel-Barthe, Head of Europe, Sanofi R&D Pharma Alliance, Management and Partnership Department

NETWORK ADVANTAGE

NETWORK ADVANTAGE

How to Unlock Value from Your Alliances and Partnerships

By Henrich Greve, Tim Rowley
and Andrew Shipilov

JB JOSSEY-BASS™

A Wiley Brand

Under the Jossey-Bass imprint, Jossey-Bass, 989 Market Street, San Francisco CA 94103–1741, USA www.josseybass.com

Registered office

John Wiley & Sons, Ltd, The Atrium, Southern Gate, Chichester, West Sussex, PO19 8SQ, United Kingdom

For details of our global editorial offices, for customer services and for information about how to apply for permission to reuse the copyright material in this book please see our website at www.wiley.com.

Wiley publishes in a variety of print and electronic formats and by print-on-demand. Some material included with standard print versions of this book may not be included in e-books or in print-on-demand. If this book refers to media such as a CD or DVD that is not included in the version you purchased, you may download this material at http://booksupport.wiley.com. For more information about Wiley products, visit www.wiley.com.

Designations used by companies to distinguish their products are often claimed as trademarks. All brand names and product names used in this book are trade names, service marks, trademarks or registered trademarks of their respective owners. The publisher is not associated with any product or vendor mentioned in this book. This publication is designed to provide accurate and authoritative information in regard to the subject matter covered. It is sold on the understanding that the publisher is not engaged in rendering professional services. If professional advice or other expert assistance is required, the services of a competent professional should be sought.

Library of Congress Cataloging-in-Publication Data is available

A catalogue record for this book is available from the British Library.

ISBN 978–1–118–56145–4 (hbk)   ISBN 978–1–118–56138–6 (ebk)
ISBN 978–1–118–56140–9 (ebk)

Set in 11/15 pt ITCGaramondStd-Bk by Toppan Best-set Premedia Limited
Printed in Great Britain by TJ International Ltd, Padstow, Cornwall, UK

Table of Contents

Acknowledgments

This book is the product of a discussion among colleagues of what we do well at INSEAD. One of the answers was that we understand the role of networks in business. Another is that we can bridge the research we do and the practice that we teach. The discussion made Andrew and Henrich think about writing this book, and we immediately realized that we needed Tim on board as well. The teamwork that spanned Singapore, France, and Canada has been a great part of writing the book.

Even with three authors, we owe debts to others. This book contains not just our ideas, but those of numerous other academics, who have written research articles, discussed their work with us, commented on our work, and asked interesting questions. We reference their intellectual contributions in the book in deference to their stimulating insights.

Rosemary Nixon at Wiley supported our project from the beginning and has been a great help through the process. Our writing has benefited from the generous, creative, and thorough advice of Katherine Armstrong and Marianne Wallace. Michelle Ie has produced the graphics and helped with the fact checking. Anne-Marie Carrick has helped with interviews. And Matt Fullbrook has helped with several examples.

INSEAD and the Rotman School have supported us throughout. In addition to providing us time, INSEAD supplied funding for the book-writing project. Both schools have made possible the conversations with colleagues and executives that inspired us as we worked on the ideas for this book. In particular, we benefited from conversations with Annet Aris, Fares Boulos, Yves Dos, W. Chan Kim, Renée Mauborgne, Bill McEvily, Yong-Kyung Lee, and Melissa Schilling.

Finally, in spite of our ambition to keep our families unaffected by this project, we do owe them debts for their patience and grace. It is important to thank our parents, Solveig and Arent, Marie and Frank, Iryna and Victor, for instilling early on the sense of intellectual curiosity that made us pursue academic careers. As researchers and teachers, we generally spend more time thinking about work than we should, even at home, so it is only natural that we thank our spouses Takako, Robin, and Ekaterina for their support.

Preface

Between 2002 and 2011, companies around the world formed close to 42,000 alliances.[1] That comes out to about 4,000 per year—a lot of time, energy, and money invested in collaboration. Clearly, executives and entrepreneurs believe that alliances, partnerships, and joint ventures—which we collectively refer to as "alliances"—are important tools for building competitive advantage.

As individual alliances have proliferated, firms in many industries have become connected in large "alliance networks." These networks are like a system of roads connecting cities. Each city is like a potential alliance partner. In the same way you can get to far-off destinations by going either through selected major cities or minor hamlets, your firm can reach its goals by taking certain roads to reach different alliance partners. The route you pick gives you access to many combinations of new ideas, breakthrough technologies, unique resources, and smart people that may be available only in unexplored, perhaps distant, parts of the network.

---

[1] Data from SDC Platinum Database owned by Thomson Reuters, accessed November 2012.

Alliance networks come in different configurations. For some industries the network might resemble a dense spider web of highways connecting clusters of cities. In other industries, the network is very fragmented with highways linking many otherwise unconnected cities through one main city hub. The shape of the alliance network matters for innovation and competition in the industry.

Firms have different positions in the alliance network. Some firms are found in dense clusters of companies that all have ties to each other. Other firms exist at the center of a spider web of firms that connect to them but not to each other, others are at the edge of the web, and yet others are isolated. A firm's position in the alliance network matters greatly for its success. And the configuration of your network matters for the competitive future of your firm.

Bridging the Gap between Academics and Executives

We wrote this book as a result of an observation we made while collectively reflecting on our alliance research and our experiences teaching executives: there is a gap between how academics and managers see alliances. Extensive research by academics in management, sociology, and economics illustrates that alliance networks are conduits across which information, power, and cooperation flow. These studies show that firms extract competitive advantage from their positions in alliance networks. However, most managers are unaware of the competitive advantages available in alliance networks and are instead preoccupied with capitalizing on the advantages gained from single alliances. They see the individual roads (alliances) from their perspective, but they don't observe how all of the alliances their companies have formed actually work together (the alliance portfolio). And they certainly don't see the whole map (the alliance network).

This myopic focus on individual roads and not on exploring the broader map prevents countless executives from understanding how they can benefit from alliance networks. Having identified this gap, we want to share our research with managers to help them generate greater returns from collaboration by shifting their perspective from single alliances to the more comprehensive alliance network surrounding their companies. By reading this book you will see how your firm can achieve the *network advantage*: gaining more information, cooperation, and power from your alliances and your firm's position in the alliance network as compared to your competitors.

Our Perspectives

Collectively, the three of us have spent 40 years doing research on alliances. Together, we've published findings from nearly 30 studies on alliances in leading academic journals. We've interviewed numerous executives and taught hundreds of executive program participants at INSEAD (France/Singapore/Abu Dhabi) and the University of Toronto. Over several decades we've studied alliances in a variety of industries including investment banking, global shipping, steel, and semiconductor manufacturing. We're also familiar with research done by our colleagues who have studied alliances in many other contexts including telecommunications, pharmaceuticals, and information technology. And, as editors of academic journals that publish alliance research, we've also helped shape the evolution of the new knowledge on alliances.

Unfortunately, academics (ourselves included) don't usually do a good job translating what we know about the business world to the executives who operate in that business world and who need this knowledge to drive value. In turn, executives probably never read our journals, and rightly so. Most academic journals are not written for executives. In this book, we seek to do a better job translating and communicating the key insights academics have discovered about alliance networks that can help managers improve alliance success and their competitive advantage.

Increasing Your Network Advantage

This book is intended for managers who are concerned with generating competitive advantage and maximizing the benefits from their alliances. If you are a business executive whose company has alliances with customers, suppliers or competitors, then this book is for you. If you don't have such relationships but are considering forming them in the future, then this book is for you as well. Any executive thinking about how to build network advantage needs to understand the rationale behind his/her alliance portfolio, its position in the overall industry's network, and whether both of these are aligned with the firm's strategy. In this book, we refer to organizations as "firms," but our advice is valuable for other organizations such as NGOs, hospitals, not-for-profits, or educational institutions. Finally, this book is for entrepreneurs. More than other types of companies, many young and/or small ventures succeed chiefly by accessing resources through alliances. Entrepreneurs lack deep pockets, sit outside established industries and need to do more with less. They have to be highly strategic about alliances, because their competitive advantage is directly related to alliance networks.

We know that many managers are frustrated by their experiences with alliances. Over 50% of alliances fail and these failures erode their companies' competitive advantage. It's common to place blame on the other alliance partners: those who must have had the wrong resources or culture, were not very trust-worthy, or were not willing to cooperate fully. Some managers say they were just plain unlucky.

The somewhat myopic mentality of many managers masks a bigger issue. The firm's network advantage does not simply depend on each individual alliance in isolation. The benefits reaped from an individual alliance depend on the other alli-ances surrounding the firm—its alliances with other partners, its partners' alliances with other partners, and the overall net-work of alliances. So, despite a firm's best efforts to form a cooperative and mutually beneficial alliance, it may still not meet expectations. By understanding how each individual alli-ance fits into a broader alliance network, managers will reduce the failure rate of their alliances. It might not be bad luck or bad timing that takes you down, but a bad alliance portfolio and a bad position in your alliance network.

The Toolbox

This book is full of tools and concepts based on our own research published in academic journals as well as research done by colleagues we admire. We present an overview of each tool within the book and then collate them in Appendix Two for easy use and reference later on. The tools will help you evaluate whether you have the correct alliance portfolio and whether you have the right position in your industry's alliance network. We can help you understand where competitive advan-tages lie in your alliance network and how you can change both your portfolio and your network position if you find that they are not right for your strategy. The tools will also help you think through your existing alliances and see whether there are new sources of competitive advantage that you can discover by recombining your existing partners' knowledge, experience, and resources.

We tested and refined these tools in executive education classrooms in Europe, Asia, the Middle East, and North America. We collected many case studies through which we will translate the key academic findings. Some of these cases come from studies published in major academic journals or teaching case libraries, while others were shared with us by our executive program participants.

Benefits For You

By the time you finish reading this book, you may be challenging your assumptions about managing alliances and partnerships. If you're an executive in a firm that has never had a particular alliance strategy, you may have developed a foundation for one. If you're unsure of what your alliance portfolio should look like, you'll see that we've provided the tools to help you design it. If you're stuck in the wrong alliance portfolio, the book will provide you with ideas on how to change it. If you're suffering from lack of partners, you may be surprised to see that there are multiple ways to increase your attractiveness to them. If you run a large organization and think you're too busy to set up specialized operations for managing alliances, we'll show you that it's not that difficult to do.

From our research we know that there are executives and entrepreneurs who intuitively understand how to achieve network advantage. They get new ideas, better information, or unique resources from their alliance networks. This knowledge gives them the edge over their competition. Good news! This knowledge need not be for the chosen few; it can be learned and taught. We invite you to read the book, use the tools, and unlock your own network advantage.

Introduction: All Roads Lead to London

History teaches us that position is important. Imagine you've been transported back in time to the Roman province of Britannia in year 150 AD. You meet a Roman soldier and ask: "Where do the roads lead to on this island?" His answer is not Rome, but rather "Londinium" (London), a city which was founded around 50 AD and within a hundred years became a central connecting point for the major roads in the region (see Figure I.1). Londinium was connected by main routes to Durovernum (Canterbury), Noviomagus (Chichester), and Calleva (Silchester Roman Town), all key cities in the production and distribution of important resources. These cities provided road access to the major military bases of Eburacum (York) and Deva (Chester) and to major transportation hubs such as Dubris (Dover).[1] Sitting on the waterway later to be named the Thames River, Londinium was a central hub in the vast and growing network of transportation routes which gave it an advantage over other cities. Because all roads led to Londinium, it had better access and control over the flow of resources.

---

[1] http://simple.wikipedia.org/wiki/Roman_roads_in_Britain.

Figure I.1: All roads lead to London

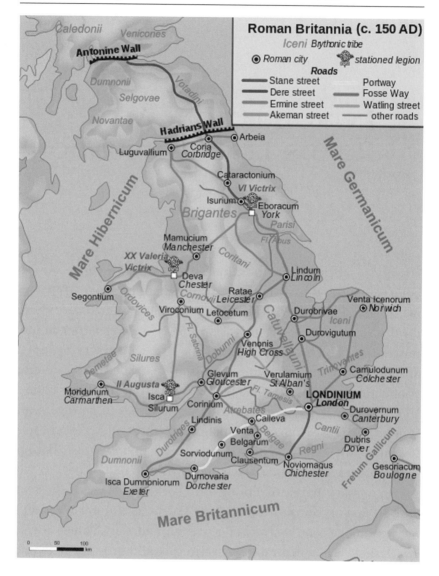

This also holds true for alliances, which work in the same way as roads connecting cities. Alliances can be defined as enduring and formalized collaborative relationships between two firms that involve significant exchange of information and resources. We make this definition intentionally broad and include "strategic alliances," "joint ventures," and "partnerships" within it. Our definition also includes any enduring buyer–supplier, joint manufacturing, R&D, or licensing agreements between firms. Because alliances are collaborative relationships, we refer to firms connected through them as alliance partners or simply partners. The traffic between partners includes the exchange of ideas, technologies, resources, and people. All of the alliances a firm has with its partners represent the firm's alliance portfolio.

In Ancient Rome, building and maintaining roads was an important government task—survival of the state depended on it. The Empire needed roads to move troops and military supplies and to facilitate communication, trade, and the transport of goods. The road network was a source of advantage: good quality roads, routes leading to many other cities, and shortcuts which provided faster access to resources in other regions, were key ingredients for prosperity and growth. Cities with these characteristics enjoyed greater flows of commerce and information across the Empire and were better able to mobilize forces against rebellion uprisings.

Just as the prosperity of individual cities in Roman Britannia depended on their position in the network of roads, your firm's prosperity depends on its position in an *alliance network*—the system of alliances that interconnects all firms within your industry and beyond. Your firm can unlock three key advantages from its alliance network: information, cooperation, and power.

- **Information** exchanged through the network can provide your firm with ideas for product or service innovation, sources of operational efficiencies, or opportunities for finding new customers.

- **Cooperation** with partners in the network, through pooling resources or knowledge to achieve resource-sharing synergies or joint learning with them, enables your firm to benefit from the assets and expertise of others.
- **Power**, your ability to influence your partners and make them do what you want them to do, allows your firm to structure the activities of the alliances and influence the allocation of rewards.

In short, **alliance networks affect your firm's ability to achieve competitive advantage**. And because firms occupy different positions within their alliance networks, these positions become sources of competitive advantage for some and sources of disadvantage for others. The firms that discover and unlock the hidden potential in their alliance networks achieve the greatest advantages.

Intuitively, we can understand the importance of road networks for the prosperity of cities. However, many executives we speak to don't understand the importance of alliance networks for the prosperity of their companies. To be fair, they do understand the importance of individual alliances and say that these alliances are important. This is why firms around the world formed close to 42,000 alliances over the past decade. But, when executives refer to "alliances," they almost exclusively mean relationships with individual partners and they seldom think about how all of their firms' relationships fit together. Nor do these executives actively manage these networks to extract the competitive advantages within them. A Director of Corporate Alliances at Unisys validated this by saying "I don't think that we spend a lot of time thinking how our [alliance] network works today. In most cases, worrying about how [individual relationships] fit within a larger network isn't something we've spent a lot of bandwidth on."[2] We recently spoke with a senior executive from another multinational firm who confirmed that "even if we can map our alliance network and see where our firm is, we still don't know how to use this knowledge."

Let's go back to our road analogy. Focusing on individual alliances and not seeing the importance of a firm's position in an alliance network would be the equivalent of attributing Londinium's eminent role in Britannia's road network solely to the one road connecting Londinium to the city of Calleva (now only an archaeological dig).[3] This would ignore Londinium's additional benefits of having roads that led to major military encampments in York and Chester or to other transportation hubs such as Dover. It would also fail to recognize the value of the goods and information traveling from Calleva not only to London but also to other cities in the province.

When you take a myopic view and concentrate only on your firm's individual alliances, you miss the opportunity to capitalize on the additional information, cooperation, and power inherent in the broader network of alliances surrounding your firm. By aligning the structure of your alliance portfolio with your strategy and by using your firm's position in the alliance network, you can maximize the value of your individual alliances and generate greater competitive advantage. In other words, **your network position becomes a distinct**

---

[2] Lavie, D. and H. Singh. 2012. The evolution of alliance portfolios: The case of Unisys. *Industrial and Corporate Change* 21(3): 763–809.

[3] http://en.wikipedia.org/wiki/Calleva_Atrebatum.

source of competitive advantage. We call this the "network advantage."

Three Degrees of Network Advantage

Throughout the book, we will use three different perspectives to think about a firm's network advantage. Imagine you're examining your firm's position in its alliance network by looking through a microscope where you can adjust the lens (and degree of magnification) to expand or reduce your field of vision. This same approach applies when looking at digital road maps. You can zoom in to see the individual street-level perspective or zoom out to see the broader city or country map. Figure I.2 provides a useful image of the three perspectives you

Figure I.2: Three degrees of network advantage

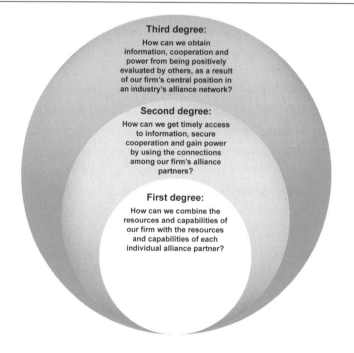

Third degree:
How can we obtain information, cooperation and power from being positively evaluated by others, as a result of our firm's central position in an industry's alliance network?

Second degree:
How can we get timely access to information, secure cooperation and gain power by using the connections among our firm's alliance partners?

First degree:
How can we combine the resources and capabilities of our firm with the resources and capabilities of each individual alliance partner?

can see using this imaginary microscope. We call these the three degrees of network advantage.

First-Degree Network Advantage

If the relationships between your firm and its partners could be placed under the lens of a microscope, you (and most managers) would use the narrowest field of vision (or highest degree of magnification) to see your individual alliance partnerships—the *first-degree perspective*. At the first-degree perspective, you see only individual relationships. Therefore, your *first-degree network advantage* comes from your ability to combine your firm's resources and capabilities with the resources and capabilities of each individual alliance partner. For these relationships, two key factors contribute to first-degree network advantage: partner compatibility and partner complementarity. *Compatible partners* trust each other and have similar skills and routines that make it easy to work with each other; *complementary partners* bring different skills and knowledge which they combine in order to achieve their objective.

Most firms form successful alliances with complementary partners. A firm in the United States may look for a Russian partner to access markets in the former Soviet Union. An investment authority in the UAE may be looking to world leaders in the public utility sector to bring their expertise in nuclear energy to the Middle East. A biotechnology firm with expertise in developing tools for testing new drugs may seek to partner with a pharmaceutical firm to learn about how to make or market drugs.

Most alliances fail because they lack compatibility between partners. The alliance partners need to be comfortable working together. This requires the ability to form joint routines around the operations of the alliance whether this involves doing research, developing products, or producing a good or service.

Collaboration requires knowledge of what the other firm wants and willingness to supply it as well as trust that such knowledge and willingness exists on the other side.

Compatibility can fail for fairly basic reasons. In shipping, for example, some managers cite differences in quality culture as reasons not to work with another firm. Difference in quality culture simply means that the firms have different answers to the question: If something unexpected happens to a ship, how much extra cost are we willing to take on in order to deliver the goods on time? In other cases, compatibility fails because companies have vastly different formal organizational structures and policies. Imagine the difficulties a firm with a high-quality customer service policy would have when it forms an alliance with a firm that tolerates providing low-quality customer service. Our experience working with companies shows that executives responsible for making alliances spend a lot of time thinking about complementarities between partners but not enough time asking themselves about compatibility, whether or not the partners have similar or vastly different cultures that can affect how successfully they will work together.

In one research project, we studied how shipping line operators benefited from their global strategic alliances during the 17-year period 1988 through 2005. We found that these shipping firms increased their performance if they formed alliances with partners having ships of similar age. In other words, the alliances succeeded when firms with older ships partnered with firms having older ships and when firms with newer ships partnered with firms having newer ships. Similarity between the age of ships indicated compatibility between the firms' operating cultures. Were both firms willing to invest in new ships to provide superior quality service or were they comfortable operating old ships and providing lower quality service to customers? If a firm with newer ships formed an alliance with a firm having older ships, that alliance was more likely to perform poorly because these two firms had different policies on service quality.[4]

In another study, we examined how investment banks in Canada increased their share of the market for Initial Public Offerings by collaborating with other investment banks during the 38-year period 1952 through 1990. We found that investment banks with complementary partners were able to obtain a greater share in the underwriting market.[5] See Appendix One for more details about these and other studies.

The first-degree perspective is critical for building network advantage. Without the right alliance partners, ones which are both complementary and compatible, your organization will not be able to access information, cooperation, or power. If we travel back in time to Roman Britannia, Londinium generated its first-degree advantage based on its high-quality roads which led to seven nearby cities. Each of these cities traded goods and exchanged information with Londinium. A careful look at the rest of the map shows that no other city in Britannia was as connected by roads to as many neighbors as Londinium. Clearly, the quality of the roads leading out of Londinium and the willingness of its individual neighbors to trade goods and share information contributed greatly to increasing Londinium's prosperity. If a city is surrounded by bad highways leading nowhere, it will not get much information about what its neighbors do, cannot call for help, and cannot influence the decisions made by other cities. It will not thrive. The same is true of alliances.

---

[4]Mitsuhashi, H. and H.R. Greve. 2009. A matching theory of alliance formation and organizational success: Complementarity and compatibility. *Academy of Management Journal* 52(5): 975–995.

[5]Rowley, T., J.A.C. Baum, A.V. Shipilov, H. Rao, and H. Greve. 2004. Competing in groups. *Managerial and Decision Economics* 25(6–7): 453–471.

Mastering the first-degree perspective is critical for building network advantage, however, it is only the beginning. In our experience, managers tend to focus on generating and monitoring the specific benefits expected from each individual relationship, and this is where they usually stop. Investing in relationships with individual partners is necessary, but it's not sufficient to extract maximum network advantage. Working just at this level delivers only a small amount of network advantage in terms of achieving information, cooperation, and power benefits. To get the biggest network advantage, you need to expand your field of vision (change the microscope lens) to see the second- and third-degree perspectives on your alliance network.

Second-Degree Network Advantage

Let's broaden the microscope's field of vision to capture your organization's whole portfolio of alliances including alliances between partners—the *second-degree perspective*. At the second-degree perspective, you look at all of your partners in your alliance portfolio and at their connections. The *second-degree network advantage* is the unique ability to get timely access to information, secure cooperation, and gain power by using the connections among your firm's alliance partners. The extent to which your partners have alliances with one another determines the power, cooperation, and types of information flowing across the network.

Different patterns of connections can exist between you and your partners. There are three basic alliance portfolio configurations: hub-and-spoke; integrated; and hybrid. *Hub-and-spoke* is an alliance portfolio in which your firm operates at the center (the hub) and is connected like spokes in a wheel to partners that are mostly not connected to each other (see Figure I.3). *Integrated* refers to an alliance portfolio in which your firm is

Figure I.3: Hub-and-spoke alliance portfolio

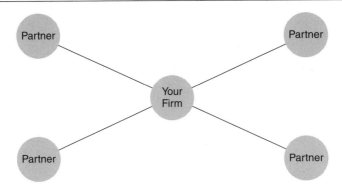

Figure I.4: Integrated alliance portfolio

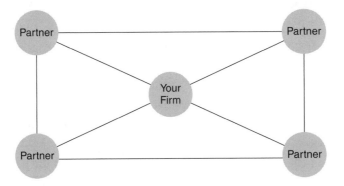

connected to partners that are also mostly connected to each other (see Figure I.4). A combination of these two types, the *hybrid*, is an alliance portfolio where your firm has some connected and some unconnected partners (see Figure I.5).

Hub-and-spoke and integrated portfolios are fundamentally different and they are used for different purposes. An integrated portfolio connects your firm to interconnected alliance partners who share the same types of information and are more likely to develop common norms around extensive exchange

Figure I.5: Hybrid alliance portfolio

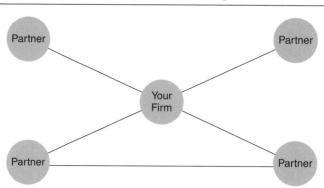

of information. This facilitates coordination and execution of complex projects as well as incremental innovation. In contrast, being at the center of a hub-and-spoke portfolio provides your firm with access to new information from each partner. It also helps your firm to engage in "brokerage"—combining ideas and resources from one partner with the ideas and resources of another partner. This portfolio is great for making breakthrough innovations.

We studied how the performance of firms in the semiconductor and steel industries was affected by the presence or absence of relationships among their alliance partners. We found that firms in the semiconductor industry performed well when they had hub-and-spoke portfolios, but firms in the steel industry performed well when they had integrated portfolios. Steel industry firms benefited from integrated portfolios because they did not need access to new information to promote breakthrough innovations. Instead their competitive advantage was based on having the ability to share incremental learning and process improvements. In contrast, firms in the semiconductor industry benefited from hub-and-spoke portfolios because they needed to combine new knowledge from different partners in order to achieve breakthrough innovations.[6] We'll return to discussing the implications of this study in subsequent chapters.

Steve Jobs was very good at building hub-and-spoke portfolios between partners that did not work with each other. Think about how he created the iPhone. He gained key knowledge about mobile phone manufacturing and how to deal with telecommunications providers through a not-so-successful collaboration with Motorola to integrate the Motorola Rokr phone with Apple's iTunes player.[7] After working with Motorola's executives, Jobs connected what he learned from Motorola to what he learned from relationships with the content providers for his AppStore and relationships with the manufacturers of the iPod. Because the AppStore content providers did not know what the mobile phone makers knew and the iPod makers did not know what these other two Apple partners knew, Jobs was uniquely positioned in the center of a hub-and-spoke portfolio. He combined all of the elements needed to make the iPhone.

A hub-and-spoke portfolio is not intrinsically better than an integrated portfolio. Sometimes a firm may need to innovate and at other times it may need to coordinate and execute. A hybrid portfolio combines the benefits of both portfolios. The more unconnected partners there are in a hybrid portfolio, the more this portfolio resembles a hub-and-spoke portfolio and the better it is for developing breakthrough innovations. The more connected partners there are in a hybrid portfolio,

---

[6] Rowley, T., D. Behrens, and D. Krackhardt. 2000. Redundant governance structures: An analysis of structural and relational embeddedness in the steel and semiconductor industry. *Strategic Management Journal* 21: 369–386.

[7] http://en.wikipedia.org/wiki/Motorola_Rokr; also see Walter Isaacson. 2011. *Steve Jobs*. New York: Simon & Schuster.

the more this portfolio resembles an integrated portfolio and the better it is for incremental innovation and project execution.

The Roman Britannia roadmap in Figure I.1 shows that Londinium had a hybrid network of roads but it was very close to a hub-and-spoke network. Except for Camulodunum (Colchester) and Durovigutum (Godmanchester), most of the other cities to which Londinium was connected did not have alternative direct roads. Because the majority of its neighbors were unconnected by direct roads, the goods and information from them had to pass through Londinium. This enabled the city to be the center of information exchange and trade among its immediate neighbors.

Third-Degree Network Advantage

By broadening the microscope lens yet again, you can expand your field of vision to the network of ties connecting all the firms in your industry and beyond—the *third-degree perspective*. The third-degree perspective looks at how your firm's partners share connections to other firms. Are your firm's partners connected to other well-connected partners? If so, your firm will be seen as a valuable partner whose opinions are worth listening to and whose products are of high quality. This broader network determines your *status*, which is defined as the perceived influence and leadership your firm has in your industry. Customers are more willing to buy products from high-status firms, and a high-status firm's suppliers are more willing to sell their products at a lower price. In short, a firm's *third-degree network advantage* is the information, cooperation, and power gained from being positively evaluated by others as a result of the firm's central position in its alliance network.

Status is an important resource for your firm and it requires time and effort to build and maintain. Recall that Canadian investment banks benefited from building relationships with complementary partners. In a different study, we also found that the higher the status of an investment bank, the more likely this bank was to increase its share of the market for Initial Public Offerings.[8] Another study showed that higher status investment banks were also able to secure capital at a lower cost.[9]

The most obvious strategy for increasing your status is to form alliances with other high-status firms. One step to make yourself attractive to a high-status partner involves investing in brand awareness, thought leadership campaigns, and increased visibility in the industry. Your firm needs to be smart about how and when it communicates with the public about its alliances with high-status partners and about its experiences as an alliance partner. You also need to establish a strong track record as a good collaborator and make it known. High-status firms will want to partner with your firm if they know that you work well with partners and help them to create value.

Londinium's high status in Roman Britannia's system of roads was driven by the fact that many of its roads led to other important towns. For example, it had connections to major transportation hubs such as Dubris (Dover), Isca Dumnoniorum (Exeter), and Glevum (Gloucester). Access to these highways meant that goods and information from important cities beyond its immediate neighborhood traveled to Londinium, further increasing its wealth and prosperity. During times of unrest, Londinium could quickly draw military help not only from the small neighboring cities but also from major military bases like Eburacum (York) and Deva (Chester), which provided needed security. Londinium's proximity to the river leading directly to

---

[8] Shipilov, A.V. 2005. Should you bank on your network? Relational and positional embeddedness in the making of financial capital. *Strategic Organization* 3(3): 279–309.

[9] Podolny, J. 1993. A status-based model of market competition. *American Journal of Sociology* 98: 829–872.

what we now call the English Channel also meant that it could be reached by ships from continental Europe. Its status was further enhanced by a visit from the Roman Emperor Hadrian in 122 AD. After this visit, Londinium made its higher status enduring by constructing impressive public buildings that reminded people about the city's special position in the province.[10]

From Academic Research to Management Practice

By developing the ability to see first-, second-, and third-degree perspectives on alliances, you begin to understand, manage, and ultimately realize network advantage.

- Finding complementary and compatible partners is your key to first-degree network advantage.
- Forming the right portfolio configuration (hub-and-spoke, integrated, or hybrid) to match your firm's strategic imperatives is the basis of second-degree network advantage.
- Building advantages associated with status is the way to realize third-degree network advantage.

Research shows that companies which are informed about these benefits and proactively managing alliance networks will achieve network advantage. We don't think these advantages are difficult to explain and understand, yet they have remained little known because of the gap between research and practice. Over the past 20 years, strategy and management journals have published tons of academic articles on the subject of network advantage. These papers represent a treasure trove of knowledge about the opportunities and threats companies face when

---

[10] http://en.wikipedia.org/wiki/Roman_London#Status_of_Londinium.

they find themselves in different types of alliance networks. Based on this research, we know how to tell different network structures apart and how they change over time. We know that some network structures help firms discover new opportunities and complex innovations. Yet, other network structures provide an inexpensive form of cooperation among firms as well as a community of trust that promotes economic exchanges and some forms of development efforts. Unlocking the advantages of building different network structures—innovations, control, cooperation, trust, and execution—requires looking beyond individual alliances. Unfortunately, the academics who write these articles, including us of course, don't usually do a good job of translating what they know about the business world to the executives who need this knowledge. Our goal in writing this book is to act as "brokers" connecting the academic and professional communities. We both have one thing in common— trying to understand how to benefit from collaboration.

How to Use this Book to Increase Your Network Advantage

We put this book together to help you increase your firm's network advantage. In Chapter 1, we'll examine in detail how shifting your field of vision between the first-, second-, and third-degree perspectives can help you understand the sources of network advantage. Using a case study on the creation of the Stealth Bomber, you'll see how one company initially failed when trying to build network advantage only to discover it 30 years later. We'll also introduce the basic concepts for how to depict alliances between companies.

In Chapter 2, we'll compare the alliance portfolios of two companies—Sony and Samsung. This chapter will help you practice shifting your field of vision (adjusting the microscope lens) between the first-, second-, and third-degree perspectives.

You'll see how Samsung was able to unlock network advantage while Sony stumbled with its alliances.

Chapter 3 focuses on how to build first-degree network advantage. You'll see how alliances help Louis Vuitton bags find their way to customers in the Middle East. Using the LVMH example, we'll examine how firms can find complementary and compatible partners. We'll also describe an analytical tool you can use to help your firm find the right first-degree partners based on strategy, resource, organization, and culture fit with them.

Chapters 4 and 5 cover how to build second-degree network advantage. Chapter 4 examines how different types of alliance portfolios can help your firm extract second-degree advantage. You'll learn how an alliance network helped a Japanese company recover from the 2011 tsunami disaster. We'll introduce the Configuration Alignment Tool which helps you think about the ideal configuration of your alliance portfolio. This means choosing whether a hub-and-spoke, integrated, or hybrid alliance portfolio best matches the requirements of your industry environment as well as your company's strategy.

Chapter 5 will provide suggestions for how you can change your alliance portfolio if it doesn't match the optimal configuration. You'll read about how a Dutch bank, Rabobank, makes money and transfers best practices in Africa and Latin America by helping local banks to form alliances with each other.

Chapters 6 and 7 are about building third-degree network advantage. In Chapter 6 we'll define status, examine its different sources, and explore the advantages high-status companies have. You'll discover what the founders of entrepreneurial start-ups can learn from Lyndon Johnson's brilliant and somewhat cruel behavior the day JFK was killed. And we'll tell you how Nestlé increased its brand awareness in South Africa by enticing customers to put giant cones on their heads and dance to the tunes of their favorite rock bands.

In Chapter 7, we'll explore how you can build your status, especially if you are a low-status firm. You'll gain knowledge of how a Danish firm succeeded in building an offshore power plant by having more alliance partners than employees. We'll introduce a tool you can use to assess your company's current status and determine how you can increase it. These two chapters contain a variety of cases about third-degree network advantage drawn from different industries and geographic regions.

Chapter 8 discusses how you should design your alliance portfolio strategy; in other words, whether you want to build a new alliance portfolio or join the portfolios created by other firms. You'll learn what Biocon, an Indian drug manufacturer, did to go from being a social pariah to the central hub in the global network of pharmaceutical alliances. This chapter may be especially interesting for entrepreneurs who are launching new organizations and don't have an existing alliance portfolio.

If your company has already built several alliance portfolios, you probably have a preferred style of alliance portfolio building. Even if your past alliances were successful, when your company faces a change in its environment or when you change your strategy, you may need to change your patterns and style of portfolio building. Chapter 9 explores how and when this should be done. You'll see how Ford Motor Company ensured its survival during the financial crisis by forming ties with its two biggest Japanese competitors . . . and why GM decided to take the punch from the crisis on its own.

Chapter 10 contains suggestions for how your firm can organize internally to achieve network advantage now and well into the future. We'll take you inside Philips Electronics and show you how this company effectively manages dozens of global alliances to bring you light, coffee, and beer.

Appendix One contains background information on some of the research published in top academic journals which inspired us to write this book and shaped the message we give.

In Appendix Two, you'll find the "Toolbox" where we've assembled templates for the five useful tools we introduce within the book. These tools will help you:

- understand the compatibility and complementarity of your individual alliances;
- think about different ways you can configure your alliance portfolio;
- visualize your status and enhance it;
- determine your strategy for making alliances; and
- discover potential alliance opportunities to pursue.

We developed these tools for teaching senior executives in North America, Europe, and Asia. Each tool is discussed within the relevant chapters. The templates in the Toolbox will allow you to use and share the tools easily later on.

Appendix Three contains a complete listing of the common names used to refer to the companies discussed in the book along with the full corporate entity names. We include this information because the research which underpins the concepts in the book was based on corporate entities. However, for ease of reading, we refer to companies by their commonly known names or shortened versions of these common names.

Going Forward

We know that all theories have limitations. You may be wondering how all of the concepts we described in this chapter play out on the ground over time. Keep reading. In the next chapter, the Stealth Bomber case study demonstrates the practical and very real link between alliance networks, network advantage, and a firm's competitive advantage.

Chapter Highlights

- Network advantage is your firm's ability to unlock information, cooperation, and power in its alliance network.
- The configuration of your firm's alliance portfolio influences how your alliance partners behave as well as the success of your partnerships.
- Unfortunately, most executives don't actively manage their alliance portfolios nor do they know how to extract competitive advantage from them.
- This book provides guidance and specific tools you can use to tap into all three degrees of your network advantage.

CHAPTER ONE

NETWORK ADVANTAGE: MAKING THE STEALTH BOMBER

Does the airplane shown in Figure 1.1 look like it can actually fly? During World War II, many in the U.S. military grappled with this question, but the XB-35 bomber, which was completed in 1948, eventually became the prototype for the B-2 Stealth Bomber that rules the air today. The development of the Stealth Bomber is a fascinating and instructive story about its creator, Jack Northrop, and the power of alliance networks.

In his time, Jack Northrop was considered to be *the* aerospace genius. He dominated aviation innovation in the twentieth century, creating a wide spectrum of aircraft which established many design principles still in use today. His most famous design was the flying wing concept, which eliminated the fuselage and was unparalleled in aerodynamic efficiency. It represented a large step forward in aviation design. In 1941, Northrop secured a contract with the U.S. military to develop his design into an aircraft that could influence the outcome and duration of World War II, but he was unable to deliver on his promise and the project was deemed a failure. It was a commercial disaster.

In 1980, Jack Northrop, then aged 85 and confined to a wheelchair, visited a secure facility to see the first B-2 Stealth

Figure 1.1: The XB-35 bomber[1]

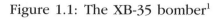

Bomber—the most advanced military aircraft capable of flying at extremely high altitudes and avoiding radar detection. Even after 40 years of technological development and use of sophisticated computer design tools, the new bomber looked like a replica of Northrop's original design. Reportedly, after seeing the aircraft, Northrop said he now realized why God had kept him alive for so long.[2]

Jack Northrop's dream was realized, but not under his watch. Now, you may think this story is about technological advancement. You may say that Northrop's project required

---

[1] Picture from http://upload.wikimedia.org/wikipedia/commons/0/0f/ XB-35.jpg.

[2] See the Aircraft Market Place blog at www.acmp.com/blog for details on Jack Northrop's flying wing design, and for more details on the Stealth program development see Thomas Withington. 2006. *B-2A Spirit Units in Combat.* Osprey Publishing; and Gary Pape and John Campbell. 1995. *Northrop Flying Wings: A History of Jack Northrop's Visionary Aircraft.* Schiffer Publishing.

technologies that did not exist at the time, but were developed long after Northrop's failed attempt. This intuition is correct, but underlying the technology, this story is actually one of alliances. It took a particular type of alliance portfolio built among several organizations to turn Northrop's dream into reality. The ultimate success of the Stealth program is a testament not only to Northrop's technological genius, but also to how alliance networks influence behavior, innovation, and performance.

A Tale of Two Attempts

Let's look at this story in more detail. The flying wing debuted in 1929. Its design minimized the aerodynamic force that opposes the plane (drag) and maximized the force that keeps the airplane in the air (lift). The intuition was that the conventional airplane fuselage creates drag and would fall down if not for the wings which create lift; the flying wing design eliminated the fuselage and was "all wing." These features gave the flying wing design a strong aerodynamic advantage as compared to the alternatives. In 1941, Jack Northrop's aviation company contracted with the U.S. Army Air Corps to transform his X216H flying wing design into a long-range bomber. The contract specified that Northrop would deliver one bomber, to be named the XB-35, by 1943 at a cost of $2,910,000 (approximate value today of $44,464,800).

Northrop's company needed help to accomplish the project and formed alliances with three organizations that had complementary resources. Table 1.1 indicates what these partners did.

Figure 1.2 shows a picture of the resulting alliance network. In later parts of this book we use computer-generated graphics to show different network structures established between different firms. However, for the analyses you will do for your own firm, you can draw simple network pictures by hand.

Table 1.1 Northrop's company alliances 1941

| Otis Elevators | Dedicated 350 draftsmen to work on design and performance issues |
| General Manufacturing
Convair | Participated in the manufacturing process and provided production facilities. Also helped solve implementation issues |

Figure 1.2: Alliance structure around U.S. Flying Wing
Bomber Program 1941–1950

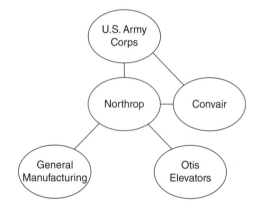

We use circles to represent firms and lines to represent alliances between them. The presence of a line between Northrop and General Manufacturing means that the two companies work with each other in an alliance. The absence of a line between General Manufacturing and Convair means that they did not have an alliance at the time of their collaboration with Northrop.

The partners soon faced obstacles. They quickly learned through the development process that maneuvering such an aircraft without a traditional tail section was difficult, and they realized that the bomb payload and range were insufficient to meet U.S. military requirements. In addition, the XB-35 project suffered from manufacturing capacity problems. Because the design required new manufacturing processes and strict engineering tolerances, Northrop maintained a relatively small manufacturing facility and a group of experts responsible for turning the design into a working bomber. While the tasks required precision, the partners also had short deadlines and ran into production issues. In the end, the project and alliances failed to overcome these problems and deliver a useable bomber on time or within budget.

The maiden voyage of the XB-35 occurred on June 25, 1946, three years after the promised delivery date and long after the end of World War II, at a cost that was 400% over budget. Not only was it late and expensive, but it was also ineffective as a bomber: the XB-35's 3,500-mile range was well below the 6,000-mile requirement. The plane couldn't carry the conventional 22,000-pound bombs. And, due to steering problems, its average bomb miss rate exceeded 3,000 meters. In 1950, the U.S. military canceled the entire program and dismantled the existing planes.

Northrop was a genius. Remember? While the first attempt was deemed a disaster, the potential of Northrop's design warranted another try, and the Flying Wing Bomber Program was resurrected in the early 1970s, well after Jack Northrop had retired. There was another noticeable difference: the number and structure of alliances among key players were more complex, which was in line with the complexity of the final product. Figure 1.3 shows the alliance network that literally took the Stealth Bomber project off the ground.

Northrop and Boeing, the companies that won the military contract, formed alliances—which we also refer to as their *ties*—for different purposes (see Table 1.2).

Figure 1.3: Alliance structure around U.S. Flying Wing
Bomber Program 1970–1989

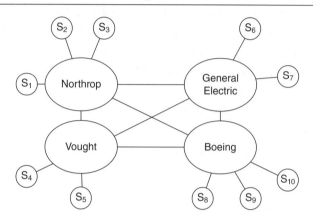

Table 1.2 Northrop company alliances 1970

Vought Aircraft	Designed and manufactured the intermediate sections of the wings
General Electric	Designed and manufactured a non-afterburner version of the F10 engine used in the F15
Boeing	Handled fuel systems, weapons delivery and landing gear

These main partners worked collectively to negotiate techni-cal standards and solve integration issues. In addition, each of these main partners formed individual ties with other subcon-tractors specific to their areas of responsibility. The result was a technical marvel. The B-2 Stealth Bomber (Figure 1.4) was capable of flying at an altitude of 50,000 feet, covering a range of 10,000 nautical miles, and was able to penetrate practi-cally any air-defense shield undetected. Two B-2 Stealth Bombers could do the work of 75 conventional aircraft. In short, it was a game changer!

Figure 1.4: The B-2 Spirit[3]

What made the second attempt so successful? Having studied alliances, we can point to the network pictures and explain how Northrop's 1940s alliance portfolio made cooperation and integration difficult. In contrast, its 1970s alliance portfolio contributed to better idea integration and fine-grained information sharing, which led to developing better manufacturing know-how. What had changed from the 1940s? Why did these ties allow more innovation to address the payload, range, and steering issues? Alliance management skills may have evolved by the 1970s, and they may have been lucky that more reasonable people were negotiating alliance terms, but we doubt such small changes would have been decisive. Instead, what had changed since the 1940s was the structure of Northrop's ties. The 1970s alliance portfolio was a key factor in fostering cooperation, and it had that effect not because of any difference in the quality of people involved in the alliances, but rather because of the structure of how these firms were connected to each other. Jack Northrop understood aviation structures, but

---

[3] Picture from http://upload.wikimedia.org/wikipedia/commons/d/dc/ US_Air_Force_B-2_Spirit.jpg.

he was unable to design an alliance network structure that could help achieve his vision.

The Principles of Network Advantage

Network advantage is actually not a complicated concept. As you've probably experienced already, networks are powerful and pervasive factors in all aspects of people's social lives. In fact, you likely make decisions every day based on your personal networks. Do you use your personal contacts to gain introductions to others who have useful information? Have you worked on a task force that brings together people with different expertise? Both situations demonstrate how to use your personal network to generate more value than would be gained from each individual relationship. No matter what kind of network, certain principles apply. We've translated these principles for use with understanding alliances. Let's put the Stealth Bomber example aside and look at how the network advantage principles apply using a person-to-person network.

Consider a study of family doctors in a small community in the United States.[4] Each doctor was asked to identify other doctors they turned to for advice, they discussed cases with, or they saw socially. The network depicted in Figure 1.5 shows the doctors' responses. Each numbered dot represents a doctor. The lines show how the doctors are connected to one another. Now, put yourself in the shoes of a senior vice president of marketing for a major pharmaceutical company which sells an antibiotic. Your life is far from easy because there is increasing regulatory pressure to curb marketing spending on specific

---

[4]We rarely study networks of persons, so for this example we use a very famous study of networks: Coleman, J.S., E. Katz, and H. Menzel 1966. *Medical Innovation: A Diffusion Study*. New York: Bobbs-Merrill.

Figure 1.5: Family doctors' advice network

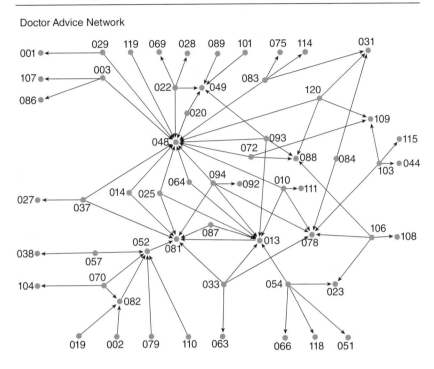

Doctor Advice Network

activities such as taking doctors to dinners and conferences. So, to influence the doctors you need to be creative.

Looking at Figure 1.5, does it provide clues for maximizing the return on your efforts to influence these doctors to write prescriptions for your company's product? Would you spend the same amount of marketing time and money on each doctor or be more discriminating? If you only had enough budget to market to a handful of doctors, which ones would you target?

Figure 1.5 can help you answer these questions by identifying the most influential doctors—those who have the greatest number of linkages to other doctors and those who have the best chance to influence the largest number of other doctors based on their positions in the network. If you already had this answer in your head, it means that you understand the basic network concept. This map of social relationships shows that some doctors have greater influence on the behaviors of other doctors in the network. Doctor #048 has 15 arrows pointing toward him, meaning he is a direct source of advice for 15 doctors. Doctors #013 and #081 have 8 such ties each. It looks like #013 has 9, but the tie between #013 and #081 is actually #013 getting advice from #081, not giving it. Assuming these doctors discuss cases involving medication choices with their peers, it would be prudent to invest a disproportionately larger amount of time and money into marketing your products to them. Knowing where in the network you can more effectively seek influence is bang for your buck and that is network advantage.

To unlock the advantages inherent in any network, it's important to understand the six key principles of network advantage which are summarized in Table 1.3 and come to life through the examples used in this chapter.

The most basic concept involves how networks provide information, cooperation, and power advantages. This is **Network Advantage Principle #1: Links among alliance partners transfer information, cooperation, and power.** This applies to work colleagues, countries, or in this case, doctors. Let's begin by looking at one of the doctors on the periphery of the network, such as Doctor #038. He has a relationship with only one other doctor, who, in turn, also has only one other relationship.

Clearly, not everyone in the network reaps the same advantages. Poor Doctor #038 has less potential for influencing others and likely is disadvantaged when it comes to accessing information flowing across the network of doctors. This illustrates **Network Advantage Principle #2: Even though networks transfer information, power, and cooperation, these**

Table 1.3 Six key principles of network advantage

#1	Links among alliance partners transfer information, cooperation, and power
#2	Even though networks transfer information, power, and cooperation, these advantages are not evenly distributed within the network
#3	Success comes to firms that actively manage their alliance portfolios
#4	It's important to recognize the different mechanisms at play in the first-, second-, and third-degree perspectives and be able to shift across these perspectives in designing your alliance portfolio
#5	Network advantage accrues to those firms which are best positioned in their alliance networks
#6	Maximum network advantage is realized when an organization coordinates its alliance activities internally

advantages are not evenly distributed within the network. That is, some network players (individuals or firms) occupy better positions than others. And that is why *network* advantages create *competitive* advantages. Some network positions are better than others.

We see similarities between the networks drawn in this chapter and the network of roads illustrated in the map of Roman Britannia shown in the Introduction (Figure I.1). Just like roads help transfer people, goods, and money between cities, relationships between firms help transfer information, cooperation, and power. And so do relationships between people. Regardless of their basis—roads, alliances, or advice—relationship networks are important. They affect cities, firms, and people, and these effects occur whether the cities, firms, or people are aware of them or not.

Alliance Portfolios

Now that you're comfortable with the concept of networks and their importance, let's return to the examples of inter-firm alliances. If you're an executive in charge of relationships in your firm, how can you benefit from your network of inter-firm relationships? The most important thing to recognize is that each alliance is a part of your alliance portfolio. How big your portfolio is, who belongs to this portfolio, and how it is configured will affect whether or not you can extract competitive advantage from your network. Let's examine what the alliance portfolio means in practice.

Business managers are very familiar with the concept of "portfolio management." Companies manage a multitude of business units through a deep understanding of not only the competitive advantage of each individual business unit but also through a clear and focused assessment of how much additional competitive advantage the collective portfolio of business units can achieve through collaboration and sharing of resources. The same is true for networks of alliances.

An organization's alliance portfolio is composed of all the "thick-line" relationships that it has with its partners. A *thick-line relationship* is one that involves both partners deeply through significant information exchange and important joint activities. In general, the thick-line relationships connecting your firm and your partners are more likely to affect your company's network advantage. You manage these relationships more closely because they involve many activities or strategic activities. The Romans paved the highways that had greater military importance or handled more commercial traffic; as a result these highways became even easier to use. Thick-line relationships between firms work the same way. It is clear that if your company has formed joint ventures or strategic alliances with a particular partner, you have a thick-line connection between your firms and they are included as a part of your alliance portfolio. When drawing pictures of alliance networks, you can use thicker lines to show these thick-line relationships and use thinner or dotted lines for the less substantial relationships like subcontractor relationships.

Sometimes a firm can have a very deep relationship with a partner, such as a buyer–supplier relationship, without calling them an alliance partner. For example, Intel and Dell don't have a global "strategic alliance" that governs all of their joint activities. However, they exchange a lot of information about product development and trends in different product or geographical markets. Intel has senior and mid-level executives whose task involves managing the relationship with Dell, and Dell also has senior and mid-level executives who manage the relationship with Intel. The two companies do joint research on trends in consumer usage of IT services.[5] Thus, for all practical purposes, the relationship between Dell and Intel will affect the network advantage of both companies and we would call them alliance partners to be considered within each company's alliance portfolio.

You should consider as an alliance any thick-line relationship that has significant resources and knowledge flowing through it and which is important to your company over the medium- to long-term horizon. Furthermore, if the relationship involves many joint initiatives and dedicated people from both organizations are involved in managing the tie, then this relationship will contribute to the network advantage of your firm.

---

[5] http://www.arnnet.com.au/article/432198/productivity_workplace _connected_it_consumerisation_study/.

Alternatively, you should not consider to be a source of network advantage any short-term buyer–supplier deal in which your company pays another company for products or services and little other information or resources follow through.

Alliance Portfolios versus Ecosystems

We are often asked about the difference between an alliance portfolio and an ecosystem, which is a popular term in modern strategic management research.[6] The definition of an *ecosystem* is very broad: a group of organizations that have a common goal. For example, the ecosystem created by Apple includes hardware manufacturers, such as Foxconn,[7] and the various companies that make apps for the App Store. Apple might have a very substantial relationship with Foxconn, which involves sharing knowledge and information. In addition to simply buying and selling the product, they have dedicated relationship managers on both sides and the relationship is important to each partner. However, app developers, especially the small ones, don't have a substantial relationship with Apple. All they do is develop apps according to Apple's specifications and place them on the virtual shelves of the App Store. Thus, from Apple's standpoint, its tie with Foxconn is a relationship worth considering as a part of its alliance portfolio. Its relationships with the app developers, especially the smaller ones, are part of Apple's ecosystem and not part of its alliance portfolio, unless some of these app developers are

---

[6] Moore, J. F. 1996. *The Death of Competition: Leadership and Strategy in the Age of Business Ecosystems*. New York: Harper Business.

[7] Foxconn is a brand owned by Hon Hai Precision Industry Company. Since Hon Hai often uses Foxconn in its external communications and even as its trading name, we use it in this book.

so important to Apple that they form a strategic alliance or a joint venture.

Thinking in terms of alliance portfolios as opposed to ecosystems should be more liberating for you. Ecosystems are usually built around large organizations such as Microsoft, Nokia, and Apple. These are the stars at the center of a galaxy. Smaller firms "orbit" the star; in other words, the center of the ecosystem. They are dependent upon the "star" firm for selling their products or services and they are also subject to the rules of the ecosystem which the "star" firm imposes. However, every firm (yours included) can become a "star" in its own right when building its alliance portfolio. That is, your firm occupies the center of your alliance portfolio. You are the center of your own alliance universe. And you should decide how to structure relationships with your partners based on your own strategic considerations. Don't let others create an alliance portfolio for you. Instead, remember to use **Network Advantage Principle #3: Success comes to firms that actively manage their alliance portfolios.**

Previously, we introduced the concept of using the first-, second-, and third-degree perspectives to think about your firm's alliance network and its network advantage. Let's return to these concepts and think about how they might have helped get the Stealth Bomber project off the ground in the 1940s.

First-Degree Network Advantage

Remember that if relationships between firms and their partners could be placed under a microscope, most managers would see the smallest component, the individual partnerships—the first-degree perspective. These are the individual relationships between a firm and its partners. In the 1940s, Northrop's alliance portfolio consisted of its individual relationships with Convair, Otis Elevators, General Manufacturing, and the U.S.

Army Air Corps. In the 1970s, its alliance portfolio was composed of relationships with General Electric, Vought, and Boeing. During the 1940s and the 1970s, Northrop formed each alliance with its partners to access necessary resources not available internally. In both time periods, Northrop created relationships to access complementary resources or capabilities.

In the 1940s, Jack Northrop had a design for the plane in his mind. Otis Elevators' expertise helped improve plane design and performance. General Manufacturing and Convair provided production facilities. In the 1970s, Northrop had the design; Vought created the intermediate sections of the wings; General Electric produced the engine; Boeing was responsible for fuel systems, weapons delivery, and landing gear. In both cases, all of the partners truly wanted to take the project off the ground and shared the same hard-charging organizational culture of American defense contractors. So, the problem in the 1940s was not one of first-degree network advantage.

Second-Degree Network Advantage

Recall that the next step to understanding network advantage is to broaden the microscope's field of vision to capture an organization's whole portfolio of alliances, including alliances between partners—the second-degree perspective. So, in moving from the first to second degree you simply add the ties between partners, as shown in Figures 1.2 and 1.3. That is, you look not only at the individual relationships between Northrop and its partners but also at how Northrop's partners themselves were connected. If a firm's partners are not connected, then the firm has a hub-and-spoke portfolio. If a firm's partners are connected, then the firm has an integrated portfolio.

The extent to which partners have alliances with one another determines the types of information, power, and cooperation flowing across the alliance portfolio. Abundant research shows that the second-degree network tells us how influence and trust flow and who is best positioned to direct that flow. The difference between Northrop's portfolios in the 1940s and the 1970s is telling. In the 1970s, there were many more ties among the main partners. Each core partner had ties to every other core partner. And this was critical to successfully turning the design into reality. In the 1970s, the flying wing bomber manufacturing process was overly complex, especially because now the developers also sought to incorporate radar avoidance. The requirements of low observability (radar avoidance) and aero efficiency meant the aircraft could have no seams and had to have precise angles to absorb and bounce radar as well as engineering tolerance tighter than those of any previous aircraft (1/10000th of an inch). With one partner designing the mid-wing section and the other designing the landing gear, for example, coordination and integration were necessary to achieve these strict engineering standards. However, these partnerships were formed among rivals who otherwise routinely competed for aviation projects. So trust and cohesiveness were not automatic to say the least. Working together was not the natural norm.

Indeed, in the late 1940s Northrop's alliance with Convair should have been a perfect match. Northrop needed to speed up production or face certain program cancellation. Convair, which initially lost the bid to Northrop, had aviation manufacturing expertise and an idle production facility that would otherwise need to be closed. Using common alliance terminology, they were complementary. However, it was not a marriage made in heaven. In fact, the project was delayed further as the two sides could not negotiate an agreeable arrangement despite desperately needing the other's help. The U.S. Army Air Corps commander, the customer, served as an arbitrator and negotiated who would control manufacturing protocols and how much production would be allocated to Convair. Ultimately, the alliances did not solve all the complex production and engineering issues.

In contrast, the main partners in the 1970s were able to collectively solve many partnership tensions and innovation problems. Perhaps the greatest challenge involved selecting a computer design system. Northrop, Boeing, and Vought each had their own CAD/CAM design systems and did not want to learn other systems. Indeed, computer-aided design and manufacturing showed great promise but was relatively new and each company was learning to use its own system more effectively. Conceding to use a partner's system would put a company at a competitive disadvantage for the next project. This conflict could have slowed down the project if not completely derailed it. But the partners came to a compromise on a common design platform because they also worked together on other related components and everyone understood that each partner had to give up its demands in some areas.

In short, in the 1970s Northrop succeeded at achieving collaboration from its partners because its alliance portfolio was more integrated. Firms that have integrated alliance portfolios are connected to partners who are also connected to each other. These portfolios resemble the spider web concentration of Northrop's 1970s portfolio more than the hub-and-spoke shape of Northrop's 1940s portfolio. Integrated portfolios connect the firm to closely linked others who share the same types of information and are more likely to develop common norms offering deep exchanges of shared knowledge.

In integrated portfolios, alliance partners are more likely to deliver on their promises. This is because information flows more freely among interconnected partners. How one firm treats a partner is easily seen by the other partners to whom both firms are connected. If one firm shirks a partner, other partners will see that and will not collaborate with the shirking firm again. The integrated relationships among the partners building the Stealth Bomber in the 1970s facilitated difficult negotiations and enhanced abilities to integrate technologies.

Additionally, integrated portfolios are beneficial for fine-grained information exchanges because multiple partners have relationships where they share a common knowledge base. This shared expertise allows them to dive deep into solving complex problems related to executing or implementing a project. However, in an integrated portfolio, working from a common information base and common views leads to similar ways of thinking that can blind partners from outside perspectives. Because partners in an integrated portfolio tend to know what the other partners know, it's unlikely that breakthrough innovations will come from such portfolios.

The alternative source of second-degree network advantage lies in a firm's alliances with disconnected partners. Being a hub in such a portfolio provides access to new information. Alliance portfolios that have a hub-and-spoke structure often have partners who know what the other partners don't. Combining ideas across such partners often leads to breakthrough innovations. Northrop had such a hub-and-spoke portfolio in the 1940s. Since it already had an innovative blueprint for the bomber, all it needed to do was to execute on the existing ideas. It needed to build reliable manufacturing systems that would effect these ideas based on incremental improvements made by multiple partners at the same time. Unfortunately, hub-and-spoke portfolios are not very good at that. Northrop got it right in the 1970s by forming an integrated alliance portfolio that fostered cooperation and tacit knowledge exchange.

Third-Degree Network Advantage

Recall that by broadening the microscope lens yet again executives can expand their field of vision to the network of alliances connecting all firms in their industry and beyond—the third-degree perspective. This broader network determines an organization's status and reputation because others consider an organization as being important if it has alliances with other important firms.

The third-degree perspective involves looking at how the partners share connections to other firms. This third-degree knowledge helps companies understand where their alliance portfolio is positioned as compared to other alliance networks in the industry and beyond, as the more centrally located alliance networks can be an extra source of resources and status in the industry. If we look back at Figure 1.3, we can see that in the 1970s the major firms—Northrop, General Electric, Vought, and Boeing—were surrounded by smaller firms, much like Londinium was surrounded by other smaller cities. The smaller firms were the subcontractors to which the major firms outsourced a lot of activities. This did not happen in the 1940s, as the major firms at the time did all the work themselves. Northrop, General Electric, Vought, and Boeing were "high-status" organizations and their subcontractors were "low-status" organizations. The status distinction reflects the influence and leadership that a firm has in its industry.

Both high-status and low-status partners need each other. High-status firms need other high-status partners in order to enforce social order in the industry. Just like we judge a person by the company she keeps, so outsiders to an industry judge a firm by the status of its partners. The fact that Northrop was able to collaborate with major industry partners such as General Electric, Vought, and Boeing signaled that Northrop was also an influential player in the industry. In the 1940s, Northrop took this to the extreme and collaborated only with high-status firms. However, when a firm needs to create new processes and technologies, only collaborating with high-status firms is treacherous because they might not have all the information and knowledge needed to make a new process or a new technology. For this, you need partnerships with low-status firms. In fact, many innovative ideas about how to make the manufacturing more efficient came to Northrop from the low-status firms.

The low-status firms were attracted to companies like Northrop in order to increase their own visibility in the industry. Companies like Northrop were attracted to low-status firms because they could outsource some lower added-value activities and also learn new things from them. The difference between Northrop's alliance portfolio in the 1940s and in the 1970s could not have been more striking: early on it simply did not have any lower status partners to work with.

Why Networks Fail

We attribute the difference between the success and failure of the Stealth Bomber program to mistakes made at the second- and third-degree perspectives. Jack Northrop already had the design for the plane. Unlike Steve Jobs, he did not need to connect vastly different worlds. All Northrop needed to do was what aerospace companies often do when working together: combine what they know, develop trust, collectively integrate their technologies, and commercialize the plane. An integrated portfolio would have been much better for this purpose than a hub-and-spoke portfolio. In both the 1940s and the 1970s, Northrop had high-status partners. However, its program succeeded in the 1970s by dividing the work between high- and low-status partners. Clearly, the difference between success and failure for major business projects has much to do with the alliance portfolios created by the companies.

Network advantage is obtained by understanding and using the first-, second-, and third-degree perspectives (see Table 1.4).

This leads to **Network Advantage Principle #4: It's important to recognize the different mechanisms at play in the**

Table 1.4 Three perspectives of network advantage

First degree	Finding complementary and compatible partners
Second degree	Building hub-and-spoke, integrated, or hybrid portfolios to match your firm's strategic imperatives
Third degree	Generating advantages associated with status which come to the well-informed and well-positioned firms

first-, second-, and third-degree perspectives and be able to shift across these perspectives in designing your alliance portfolio.

When a firm broadens its perspective to capitalize on its own position or status in the network or on the status of other firms in the network, it gains maximum network advantage. This can be summarized in **Network Advantage Principle #5: Network advantage accrues to those firms which are best positioned in their alliance networks.**

Finally, consider the last principle. **Network Advantage Principle #6: Maximum network advantage is realized when an organization coordinates its alliance activities internally.** In other words, your firm needs to have systems and processes in place that allow information sharing and coordination across the individuals and business units which are responsible for managing alliances. If one business unit learns something from a partner, it needs to transfer this learning to the other business units that manage relationships with different partners. Otherwise, the information, cooperation, and power gained from the alliance network are lost and your firm is back to the first-degree perspective—managing alliances as individual relationships and not as a part of its alliance portfolio.

Why Draw Network Pictures?

Why did we choose to draw network pictures to illustrate our points? The answer is that pictures (network pictures included) can help simplify making complex business decisions. By looking at the drawings, you could see the "big picture." By looking at the network picture of relationships between the doctors, you could see more easily which doctor was better connected than the others. And by comparing the picture depicting Northrop's alliance portfolios in the 1940s with the 1970s, you could better see how alliances between the firms actually mattered for the success or failure of the Stealth Bomber project.

By looking at different partners and their connections between each other, you can more easily see why you have a particular partner in your firm's alliance portfolio. Does it matter whether one partner works with another? If you were to introduce them to each other, what kind of collaborative projects could they pursue so that your firm benefits as well? What can you learn from one partner that you could use in your relationships with another? Is your alliance portfolio structure optimal for what you are trying to achieve? Who are the partners of your partners? Are they high or low status? Can you link to a new high-status partner by using a referral from your existing partner which already works with this firm? Network pictures help you raise these questions and engage in regular discussions around these issues. Both will help your firm be more strategic in its ability to extract network advantage.

Going Forward

In the next chapter, we provide an opportunity to practice drawing network maps and shifting your lens across the three different perspectives. This time, we are going to examine the sources of network advantage in a more contemporary competitive battle, the one that played out between the Asian giants of high technology: Sony and Samsung.

Chapter Highlights

- The six principles of network advantage are:
  1. Links among alliance partners transfer information, cooperation, and power
  2. Even though networks transfer information, power, and cooperation, these advantages are not evenly distributed within the network
  3. Success comes to firms that actively manage their alliance portfolios
  4. It's important to recognize the different mechanisms at play in the first-, second-, and third-degree perspectives and be able to shift across these perspectives in designing your alliance portfolio
  5. Network advantage accrues to those firms which are best positioned in their alliance networks
  6. Maximum network advantage is realized when an organization coordinates its alliance activities internally.
- First-degree network advantage is driven by your ability to form relationships with complementary and compatible partners.
- Second-degree advantage depends on whether your firm's partners are interconnected in your alliance portfolio. Integrated portfolios provide network advantage derived from

greater trust among partners and from facilitating the sharing of tacit information to execute projects. Hub-and-spoke portfolios provide advantage based on access to novel information for developing breakthrough innovations.

- Third-degree network advantage is driven by your firm's ability to include high-status partners in its alliance portfolio. It also depends on high-status firms' ability to learn from low-status firms.

CHAPTER TWO

COMPARING NETWORK ADVANTAGE: SONY VERSUS SAMSUNG

On April 12, 2012, the *New York Times* ran an article "Sony Revises Expected Loss to $6.4 Billion," examining the reasons for Sony's poor performance. A few weeks later on April 30, 2012, the *New York Times* published "Samsung Poised to Leave Rivals Behind," where it compared Samsung's success with the struggles of many Japanese companies, including Sony. Journalists in the second article partially attributed Samsung's outstanding performance to the superiority of its alliance strategy, especially in dealing with competitors, over Sony's. Other factors contributed, but we agree with their conclusion about alliance strategy and consider this to be a brilliant contemporary example of network advantage. In this chapter, we look beyond the headlines and demonstrate how to apply the first-, second-, and third-degree perspectives to understanding the sources of network advantage by comparing Sony and Samsung.

Between 2008 and 2011, the business press covered how both Samsung and Sony built different alliances to achieve complementarities and compatibilities with their partners. Each company had many alliance partners. Table 2.1 shows some of Sony's partnerships during this timeframe.

Table 2.1 Sony's alliances 2008–2011

Partner	Alliance objective
Hitachi	Manufacture LCD panels for use in Sony equipment
Toshiba	Manufacture LCD panels for use in Sony equipment
Sharp	Manufacture LCD panels for use in Sony equipment
Google	Install Chrome browser in VAIO computers
	Develop cloud-based products for Android platform
IMAX and Discovery Communications (three-party alliance)	Develop 3D TV platforms

Table 2.2 Samsung's alliances 2008–2011

Partner	Alliance objective
TCL Corporation	Manufacture LCD panels in China
Infineon	Manufacture chips in Germany
Korean Telecom and Intel (three-party alliance)	Transmit 3D signal over the mobile phone infrastructure

Table 2.2 shows some of Samsung's partnerships during the same timeframe.

All of these alliances combined different technologies, resources, and know-how to create new opportunities that could not be pursued by either firm on its own. Yet, we attribute

Figure 2.1: Sony's alliances, first-degree perspective

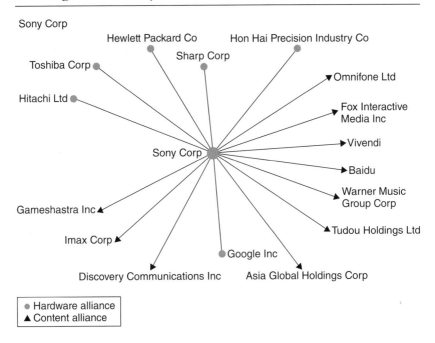

Sony Corp
Hewlett Packard Co   Hon Hai Precision Industry Co
Sharp Corp
Toshiba Corp
Omnifone Ltd
Hitachi Ltd
Fox Interactive Media Inc
Vivendi
Sony Corp
Baidu
Warner Music Group Corp
Gameshastra Inc
Tudou Holdings Ltd
Imax Corp
Google Inc
Discovery Communications Inc   Asia Global Holdings Corp

● Hardware alliance
▲ Content alliance

Sony's failure and Samsung's success not to the individual alliances they formed but rather to how they built competitive advantage using their alliance networks.

By shifting the imaginary microscope lens and broadening our field of vision, we can better understand the sources of Samsung's network advantage and Sony's network disadvantage. To do this, let's consider the alliances and partnerships Samsung and Sony formed between 2008 and 2011 (see Figures 2.1 and 2.2). As shown in Chapter 1, circles represent the companies and the lines between companies signify their alliances, which we also refer to as their ties. We will build the network pictures for the two companies in three stages, initially setting the microscope at the first-degree perspective, then expanding

Figure 2.2: Samsung's alliances, first-degree perspective

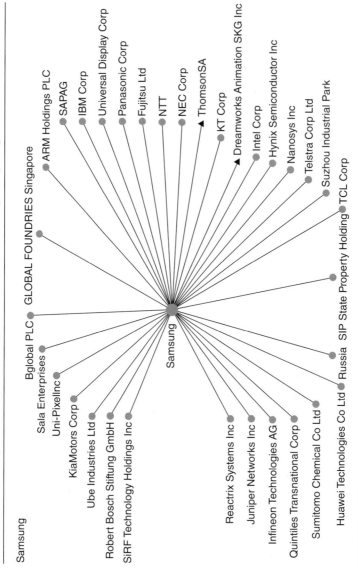

Hardware alliance
Content alliance

to include the second-degree perspective, and finally expanding to incorporate the third-degree perspective.

First-Degree Advantage

In Figures 2.1 and 2.2, we can observe each company's alliances from the first-degree perspective. Since we see only the individual alliances developed by each firm, the network itself is a bit boring: just a circle of alliance partners around the main firm. However, recall that the first-degree perspective involves examining the sources of complementarity and compatibility between the firm and its individual partners. Each firm's list of partners reflects its knowledge base which determines its opportunities and constraints for future innovations and strategies. We learn more when we also take into account the main resources that each alliance partner provides for Sony and Samsung.

From Figures 2.1 and 2.2 we see that Sony has 16 alliance partners and Samsung has 33. Since Sony has nearly half the number of partners, it appears that its history of technological excellence and past successes, such as the Walkman and PlayStation, may have given Sony the confidence to think that it could develop almost everything internally despite the rapidly changing technology industry. Unlike Sony, Samsung developed nearly twice as many partnerships, which shows that Samsung is more likely to collaborate with others. Perhaps Samsung doesn't think it has all the knowledge it needs to make new products. This may be a legacy of the fact that Samsung was late to many markets in the past, and it was always trying to catch up by acquiring knowledge and resources from more experienced alliance partners. Going back to our Roman road network analogy, compared with Samsung, Sony has fewer highways to provide the company with information, cooperation, and power. Therefore, in terms of access to new ideas, Samsung's first-degree network advantage is greater than Sony's.

Now let's look at what kinds of alliances the two firms have. This provides information about each firm's priorities and the areas of interest where they may wish to collaborate. It's not obvious from the figures, but when we looked at the rationale or objective behind each alliance we found that both companies formed alliances in two areas: electronics and entertainment. Within each of these two areas, the alliances can be classified into two categories—those developed to manufacture hardware and those developed to make use of content. In Figures 2.1 and 2.2, the content alliances for Sony and Samsung are marked by triangles on the pictures and the hardware alliances are marked by circles. So far, we can see that Sony has a lot more alliances to make use of content than Samsung, but Samsung has a lot more alliances to make hardware.

Second-Degree Advantage

In Figures 2.3 and 2.4, we can observe Sony's and Samsung's alliance portfolios from the second-degree perspective. Now we can see each firm, its alliance partners, and the alliances among its partners. Already we've moved beyond the view most managers consider. Notice how the second-degree pictures differ from the first-degree pictures. Samsung and Sony both have alliances to partners that are connected to other partners in their alliance portfolios.

In Figure 2.4, the northeast corner, we see that 12 out of Samsung's 33 partners form four clusters of connected partners (see also Table 2.3).

Overall, such connected partners are rare in the Samsung alliance portfolio. In the other three corners of Samsung's alliance portfolio, we see that the partners are mostly not connected. In fact, the number of disconnected partners is much greater in Samsung's alliance portfolio than in Sony's alliance portfolio. Therefore, we would say that Sony's portfolio is more

Figure 2.3: Sony's alliances, second-degree perspective

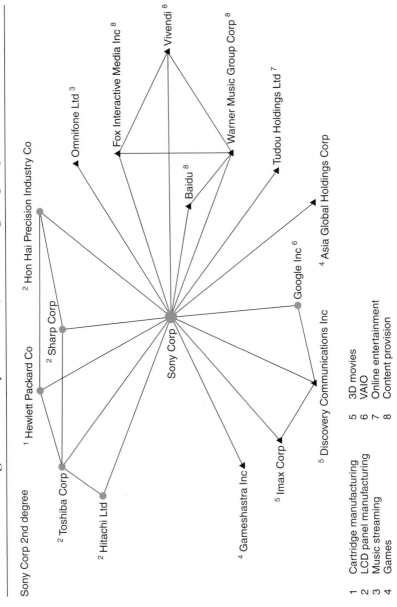

Figure 2.4: Samsung's alliances, second-degree perspective

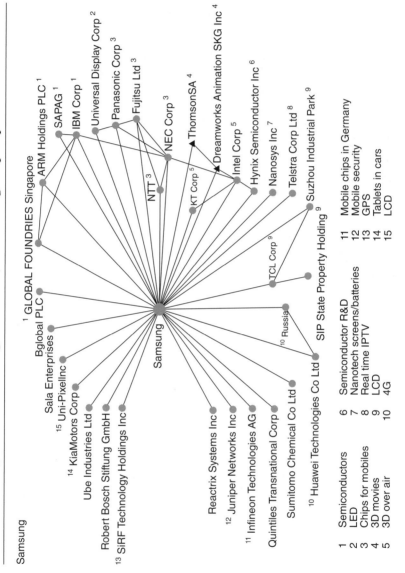

Samsung

1 GLOBAL FOUNDRIES Singapore

Bglobal PLC
Sala Enterprises
15 Uni-PixelInc
14 KiaMotors Corp
Ube Industries Ltd
Robert Bosch Stiftung GmbH
13 SiRF Technology Holdings Inc

ARM Holdings PLC [1]
SAPAG [1]
IBM Corp [1]
Universal Display Corp [2]
Panasonic Corp [3]
Fujitsu Ltd [3]
NEC Corp [3]
ThomsonSA [4]
Dreamworks Animation SKG Inc [4]
Intel Corp [5]
Hynix Semiconductor Inc [6]
Nanosys Inc [7]
Telstra Corp Ltd [8]
Suzhou Industrial Park [9]

NTT [3]
KT Corp [5]

Samsung

TCL Corp [9]

Reactrix Systems Inc
12 Juniper Networks Inc
11 Infineon Technologies AG
Quintiles Transnational Corp
Sumitomo Chemical Co Ltd
10 Huawei Technologies Co Ltd

10 Russia

SIP State Property Holding [9]

1	Semiconductors	6	Semiconductor R&D
2	LED	7	Nanotech screens/batteries
3	Chips for mobiles	8	Real time IPTV
4	3D movies	9	LCD
5	3D over air	10	4G

11	Mobile chips in Germany
12	Mobile security
13	GPS
14	Tablets in cars
15	LCD

Table 2.3 Samsung's connected partners

Partner	Alliance objective
IBM, SAPAG, ARM Holdings, GLOBAL Foundries Singapore	Semiconductors
Panasonic, Fujitsu, NTT, NEC	Chips for mobiles
Thomson SA, DreamWorks	3D movies
Intel, KT Corp.	3D over air

Table 2.4 Sony's connected partners

Partner	Alliance objective
Hitachi, Toshiba, Sharp, Hon Hai	LCD panel manufacturing
Fox, Vivendi, Warner Music, Baidu	Content provision
IMAX, Discovery Communications	3D movies

integrated than Samsung's, while Samsung's portfolio is closer to a hub-and-spoke configuration.

Many of Sony's alliance partners can also communicate with each other directly, rather than just through Sony. In Figure 2.3, we see that Sony has three clusters of connected partners (see also Table 2.4).

In contrast, many of Samsung's alliance partners communicate only with Samsung, not directly with each other. As a result, Samsung becomes the hub that collects the information generated by each of these partners. Because many of these partnerships are involved in research and development or they generate technological information as a side effect of production, Samsung receives technology-related information through its alliance portfolio. By using this new information and its own research, it can build a stronger knowledge base for future products.

Now, let's combine our understanding of the connections between Sony's and Samsung's alliance partners with our understanding of why they formed these alliances. On the alliance portfolio pictures shown in Figures 2.3 and 2.4, we've also written the rationale for each of the two companies' major alliances.

Figure 2.3 shows that the majority of Sony's hardware alliances focus on making LCD panels, which is a strategically important technology for the company. Sony is highly involved in producing LCD panel products both in large-screen formats, meaning televisions and computer monitors, and small-screen formats such as mobile phones and tablets. On the other hand, as shown in Figure 2.4, Samsung's alliances have many different purposes such as semiconductors, LEDs, chips for mobiles, 3D movies, 3D over air, LCDs, and 4G—involving both current products and technologies that may be used in future products.

If we look at the right-hand side of Sony's portfolio in Figure 2.3, we see an alliance of multiple partners that Sony works with on content provision in Asia: Vivendi, Warner, Fox and Baidu. To provide online social networking services in the United States, Sony also works with Vivendi (Universal), Warner, and Fox (as the owner of MySpace). At the southwest corner of the portfolio picture, we see that Sony also works together with IMAX and Discovery Communications to distribute 3D movie content. Sony has some content alliances with firms such as Gameshastra and Tudou Holdings, but these firms don't work with its other partners.

As shown in Figure 2.4, Samsung's alliance partners cover a broad range of technologies, but what they have in common is that Samsung has a strategic stake. Clearly, there is value for Samsung in getting access to technological knowledge and making sure that this access is unique to itself, not shared with other firms. The hub-and-spoke configuration ensures that each

Table 2.5 Samsung's alliances and learning opportunities

Partner	Alliance objective
Uni-Pixel	Next generation technologies
Universal Display Corporation	(LCD and LED screens)
TCL Corporation and Suzhou Industrial Park in China (three-way alliance)	
Juniper	Mobile security technologies
Intel	Mobile security technologies
Technicolor (owned by Thomson) and DreamWorks (three-way alliance)	Equipment for 3D movies

piece of technological knowledge is shared only with the partner who co-develops it and not with third parties.

Compared with Sony, Samsung spreads its business across many more different technologies, product lines, and partners. This allows Samsung greater access to new information which it can use to build knowledge. For example, Table 2.5 lists alliances illustrating some of these learning opportunities.

Similar to the pivotal position of Londinium (see Introduction), Samsung benefits more than Sony from being on the intersection of extra highways among otherwise unconnected partners. Samsung is able to extract more "toll charges" or second-degree network advantage from its partners in the form of better access to information or better ability to learn quickly from them.

Using the Second-Degree Perspective to Predict the Future

These alliance portfolio pictures represent not only snapshots of past decisions to collaborate; they can also be used to predict where each company's future innovations will come from.

Based on the pictures of these two companies' alliance portfolios, Sony will probably continue improving its LCD panels and perhaps find new ways of selling its content through 3D movies (IMAX/Discovery alliance) or online distribution channels (Tudou Holdings in China). It will also be able to lower the costs of its PCs by manufacturing them in cheaper locations and perhaps develop new games for its consoles. Because of the integrated nature of its alliances, most of the innovation from Sony's collaboration on LCD panels with Hitachi, Sharp, Hon Hai, and Toshiba is likely to be incremental. Sony's best chance for breakthrough innovation will come from combining LCD knowledge with PC manufacturing, gaming, and Internet TV.

Because Samsung has a hub-and-spoke portfolio, it has a much wider space for technological innovation. It can combine solutions from R&D on memory chips (alliance with Hynix Semiconductor) with solutions on mobile security (alliance with Juniper Networks) as well as combine ideas on how to stream TV broadcasts to mobile devices (alliance with Telstra) with an understanding of how to transmit 3D high-definition images over the air (alliance with KT and Intel). On top of that, Samsung can neutralize Sony's advantage in manufacturing LCD panels via an individual alliance with TCL Corp and make footholds into Sony's content market through its three-way alliance with DreamWorks Animation and Technicolor (Thomson).

Samsung's alliance with Universal Display Corporation (UDC) is an example of an alliance that provides second-degree advantage based on the hub-and-spoke configuration. This alliance was created to develop active matrix organic light-emitting diode materials used in next generation displays. UDC doesn't know what Samsung is learning about displays from the alliance it developed with Nanosys to use nano technology in screens and batteries. Nor does UDC know what Samsung is learning from its alliance with Uni-Pixel to manufacture optical shutters also to be used in screens. And none of these partners knows what Samsung is learning in its three-way alliance with TCL and Suzhou Industrial Park, created to manufacture screens. These alliances provide Samsung with access to new types of thinking, information, and solutions.

It's clear that Samsung is more than just a television and chip maker, but rather a company that develops cutting-edge products by combining technologies from different domains. Samsung's current profit driver is the Galaxy series of tablets and mobile phones, but we might expect to see some form of 3D HD portable devices hitting the market very soon. These may be incorporated into automobile electronics through its alliance with Kia Motors. Overall, since Samsung's alliance portfolio has more unconnected partners than Sony's portfolio, we anticipate seeing more breakthrough innovations from Samsung in the foreseeable future.

Third-Degree Advantage

Figures 2.5 and 2.6 show the alliance portfolios of Sony and Samsung from the third-degree perspective. Now, in addition to the ties with and among the partners of each firm (second-degree perspective), we can also see the broader network of ties each firm's partners have to other partners in the industry and possibly in other industries. This third-degree perspective shows that the firm's overall ties matter because they help the others to judge the firm's status. As we will discuss more fully in Chapter 6, a firm's status is the perceived level of leadership and influence it has in its industry. The more connected a firm is to well-respected firms, the higher its status. Well-respected firms are usually the well-connected firms, like the city of Londinium was in Roman Britannia. The result is a self-fulfilling prophecy where the well-connected firms find it easier to get new alliance partners, and those who lack connections have

Figure 2.5: Sony's alliances, third-degree perspective

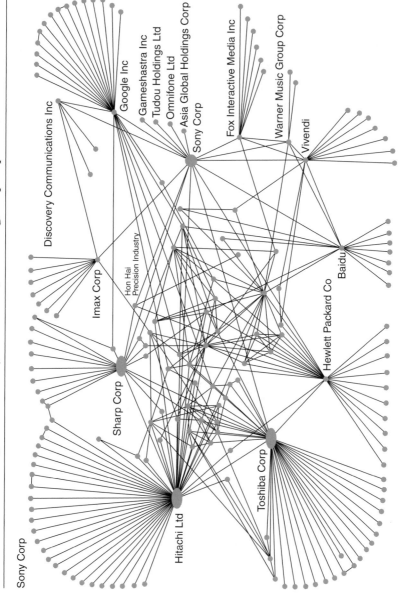

Figure 2.6: Samsung's alliances, third-degree perspective

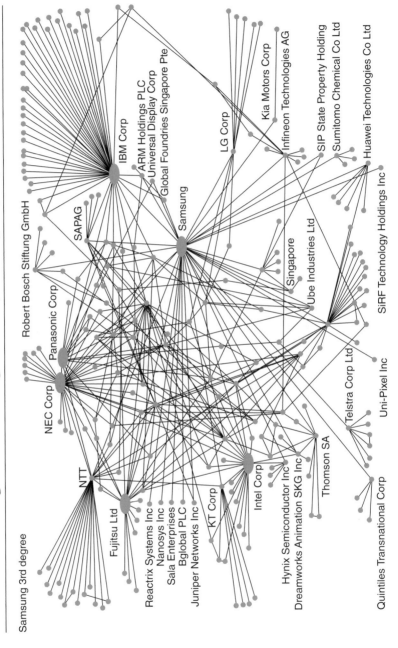

Samsung 3rd degree

Robert Bosch Stiftung GmbH

IBM Corp

ARM Holdings PLC
Universal Display Corp
Global Foundries Singapore Pte

SAPAG

Samsung

LG Corp

Kia Motors Corp

Infineon Technologies AG

SIP State Property Holding

Sumitomo Chemical Co Ltd

Huawei Technologies Co Ltd

Panasonic Corp

Singapore

Ube Industries Ltd

NEC Corp

SiRF Technology Holdings Inc

NTT

Telstra Corp Ltd

Uni-Pixel Inc

Fujitsu Ltd

Reactrix Systems Inc
Nanosys Inc
Sala Enterprises
Bglobal PLC
Juniper Networks Inc

KT Corp

Intel Corp

Thomson SA

Hynix Semiconductor Inc
Dreamworks Animation SKG Inc

Quintiles Transnational Corp

difficulty getting any. It may seem that firms need to find only high-status partners. However, in the turbulent industries where innovation is highly uncertain but vital to survival, firms also need to collaborate with low-status partners because they are usually the sources of innovation.

Figure 2.5 shows the third-degree perspective on Sony's network. The size of each oval represents the status of each firm, which is driven not only by their direct relationships but also by the relationships their partners have with their own partners. To make the picture easier to read, we did not show all of Sony's partners' ties. Figure 2.5 shows that most of Sony's partners in hardware, such as Hitachi, Sharp, and Toshiba, have higher status than Sony. As a result, they depend less on Sony than Sony depends on them. Recall that Sony bets its future in hardware manufacturing on collaboration with these firms in the area of LCD displays. But alliances with Sony represent a small part of the networks of these higher status partners. In negotiating with these partners, Sony doesn't have the bargaining power, nor does it have many alternative sources to turn to for its supply of hardware. Additionally, since Sony doesn't have lower status partners in its hardware manufacturing network, it doesn't have access to innovative ideas on how to make hardware.

Take a look at Figure 2.6. You'll see that Samsung's key partners—IBM and Intel—have high but equal status to Samsung. These partners depend on Samsung as much as Samsung depends on them. NEC commands high status because it has many alliances with high-status partners. However, high status does not always guarantee success. The alliance formed between NEC, NTT, and Samsung to develop semiconductors for smartphones actually failed three months after its announcement, and many observers cited slow decision making at NEC and NTT for this failure. Looking at our picture it becomes clear that NEC and NTT were involved in so many alliances that it was probably difficult for them to devote time and effort to the alliance with Samsung.

In hardware, Samsung also has low-status partners such as Nanosys and Uni-Pixel, which depend more on Samsung than Samsung depends on them. Ultimately, ties to firms like IBM and Intel allow Samsung to collaborate with equal and high-status partners and signal its influence to the rest of the industry. Its ties to firms like Nanosys and Uni-Pixel allow Samsung to bring ideas from the periphery of hardware development which will make Samsung more innovative.

Looking Inside the Circles

A firm's internal management and organizational structure can have a big impact on whether the firm maximizes network advantage. If we opened the circles that represent Sony and Samsung on our maps and looked inside at their internal organization and business processes, we would see that these companies are managed very differently.[1] These differences matter for the firms' ability to achieve network advantage. Sony and Samsung are similar in that they both have a product-based organizational structure, but the similarity ends there.

To continue with our Roman road network analogy, Londinium benefited from an internal street network planned for easy internal movement of goods and people. Samsung also had this kind of internal structure which allowed the information, cooperation, and power received from alliance partners to easily travel inside Samsung. In contrast, Sony had many high walls between its departments with very few access gates, so the information, cooperation, and power received from alliance partners got stuck inside its organization.

---

[1] Chang, S.J. 2008. *Sony vs. Samsung: The Inside Story of the Electronics Giants' Battle for Global Supremacy*. John Wiley & Sons, Ltd.

Sony: Divisions Rule

Let's take a look at Sony's internal management and organizational structure. In 2007, Sony had two content businesses—Sony Music Entertainment and Sony Pictures Entertainment—which were completely independent corporations with limited supervision from the company's headquarters.

The rest of Sony's organization consisted of nine hardware divisions including:

- TV
- Video
- Audio
- Digital Imaging
- VAIO
- Semiconductors
- Core Components
- Connect
- Business and Professional

During the 1990s and 2000s, a series of reorganizations shifted a lot of authority and accountability to individual divisions from Sony's headquarters. Individual divisions were compensated for their performance based on division-level income statements and balance sheets, which encouraged short-term efficiencies at the expense of reducing long-term investments. These divisions also had to incur their own research and development (R&D) costs because the centralized R&D function (including managing alliances) was shifted to them. These changes discouraged divisions from making investments that would benefit other divisions. Before the restructuring, R&D was done at the group level and it produced radically new products for Sony such as the Walkman and the PlayStation. In contrast, division-level R&D focused on producing new products and managing alliances only for individual divisions. Since the 1990s, this combined narrow focus on short-term efficiencies and shifting of R&D to the division level might have prevented Sony from introducing radically new products.

An even bigger chasm existed between the hardware and content businesses. Not only were they operated from different continents, but also the interests of the hardware and content businesses often diverged. For example, illegal music sharing, which started in the 1990s, was a disaster for the content division, but it encouraged people to buy more powerful hardware, which was a boon for the hardware division. Sony failed to out-gun Apple for a number of reasons, most notably because Sony's content business felt that music could not be given away at a low price; yet this strategy formed the core of Apple's success.

As a result, information sharing across Sony's two major silos—hardware and content, as well as inside the hardware division itself—was very low. Consequently, the company's executives could not understand how they could leverage the alliances of both divisions to achieve network advantage. The information, cooperation, and power that hardware alliances could have provided were also not leveraged by the content division, and vice versa. By the time the different divisions were forced to cooperate and extensively share information from alliances, Sony had lost its lead in two crucial categories: televisions and portable music devices. Competitors had beaten Sony in the race to flat-panel displays and digital music players like the iPod.[2]

Clearly, its organizational structure and conflicting incentives made it difficult for Sony to create synergies across different functional units. Headquarters could also have done more

---

[2] http://www.nytimes.com/2012/04/15/technology/how-sony-fell-behind-in-the-tech-parade.html.

to help the firm achieve network advantage. For example, they could have promoted better cooperation and resource sharing between divisions as well as greater transfer of alliance learning across divisions. The company did not have a well-functioning and centralized alliance management function that could have trained executives to extract value from collaborations. Additionally, the company was not very good at looking outside to begin with. And headquarters did nothing to correct this problem.

Samsung: Strong Center Connects Divisions

Samsung also had a divisional structure, but the nature of communication between the different divisions was different. Employees at Samsung are fiercely loyal to the organization as a whole. Unlike Sony's divisions, business units in Samsung don't report separate balance sheets and income statements. All business units report to the Office of Secretaries, which was formerly called the Group Strategic Planning Office. This HQ-level body oversees all major financial, strategic, public relations, and HR decisions. Because of the intervention of this coordinating body, divisions within Samsung are able to share resources and to create synergies.

In order to ensure cooperation across divisions, Samsung also runs cross-business teams. One example is the Digital Solutions Team, which develops digital convergence or network products. Even though divisions compete with each other, they often provide mutual assistance. For example, when the memory business experienced huge losses, it was supported by the home appliances and telecommunications divisions. Business units also closely collaborate when they develop new products. Ultimately, better information sharing and internal coordination across business units help Samsung to transfer the knowledge and resources which it obtains across different alliances with different partners.

Comparing Network Advantage: Sony vs. Samsung

In Table 2.6 we've provided a summary of the Sony vs. Samsung comparison. Seen from a first-degree perspective, they are similar except for Samsung's greater willingness to collaborate with partners. Seen from a second-degree perspective, the greater integration of the Sony portfolio is clear, and it has consequences for its innovation opportunities and network advantage. Finally, Samsung has a greater span of status in its partners, and none of its close collaborators have greater status than it does.

Going Forward

Now that you have experienced the differences between the first-, second-, and third-degree perspectives on network advantage and have seen the need for internal coordination to realize network advantage, let's examine each of these perspectives in detail. In the next several chapters, we introduce tools you can use to evaluate and enhance your firm's first-, second-, and third-degree network advantage.

Chapter Highlights

- Even firms that are similar at the first-degree perspective, like Sony and Samsung, can have widely differing network advantages because their alliance portfolios are different from the second- and third-degree perspectives.
- At the second-degree perspective, the Samsung and Sony alliance portfolios are different because Samsung has more unconnected "spokes" in its hub-and-spoke portfolio, while Sony's portfolio is much more integrated. The hub-and-spoke configuration of Samsung has helped it make more breakthrough innovations, while Sony has been left making incremental improvements.

Table 2.6 Sony vs. Samsung network advantage comparison

	Sony	Samsung
First-degree perspective:		
Complementary and compatible partners	Yes	Yes
Number of partners	16	33
Willingness to collaborate	Lower	Higher
Second-degree perspective:		
Portfolio configuration	Hybrid, but close to integrated	Hybrid, but close to hub-and-spoke
Unconnected partners	Only 6 out of 16 partners (37.5%) Fewer than Samsung	22 out of 33 partners (67%) More than Sony
Connected partners	10 partners in 3 clusters (62.5%)	12 partners in 4 clusters (36%)
Innovation opportunities	Incremental innovation potential in hardware due to large clusters of integrated partners Radical innovation potential across content and hardware due to unconnected partners	Breakthrough innovation potential in a wide variety of areas

Third-degree perspective:

High-status partners

Sony's main hardware partners have higher status than Sony, so Sony depends more on them than they do on Sony	Samsung has more relationships with equal status partners; no partners have much higher status than Samsung

Low-status partners

Sony lacks low-status partners in the rapidly changing hardware industry to draw ideas from	Samsung has more low-status partners in the hardware industry to draw innovative ideas from
In content, Sony has a few low-status partners and smaller status differences that may allow greater collaboration	

Internal organization:

Organizational structure features independent divisions and conflicting incentives which discourages information sharing across divisions	All divisions report to strong central Office of Secretaries
No centralized alliance management function	Office of Secretaries connects divisions and promotes sharing information through cross-business teams (e.g. Digital Solutions Team)
Internal organization doesn't encourage different divisions to collaborate and share information from different alliances	Internal organization allows transfer of information, knowledge, and resources across its different alliances

- At the third-degree perspective, Sony and Samsung's networks are also different because Sony's main hardware partners have higher status than Sony, and they don't depend on Sony as much as Sony depends on them. Samsung has partners with high (but equal) status to Samsung as well as low-status partners from which it can draw innovative ideas. This too leaves Samsung better poised to make breakthrough innovations than Sony.
- Internally, Sony's organization doesn't encourage different divisions to collaborate and share information from their alliances. Samsung's divisions share a lot of information, which allows it to transfer information, knowledge, and resources across its different alliances. Like Samsung's alliance portfolio, its internal organization is geared toward breakthrough innovations.

CHAPTER THREE

THE FIRST-DEGREE PERSPECTIVE: STRENGTHENING THE FOUNDATION OF NETWORK ADVANTAGE

Imagine yourself sitting on the veranda overlooking the cosmopolitan metropolis of Dubai wearing haute couture clothing, sipping fine champagne, and glancing at your expensive watch. Chances are very good you're enjoying these high-end products as a result of the Chalhoub Group's alliance with LVMH. Chalhoub, a highly successful purveyor of luxury goods,[1] has relationships with retailers and clients across 14 countries in the Middle East region. Its business model involves providing companies that produce luxury brands in Europe and North America with access to the Middle Eastern markets. Chalhoub sells products from these companies in the Middle East, either through its own retail stores or through retail partners. One of

---

[1]This part of the chapter is based on publicly available information as well as on the INSEAD case study "Moët Hennessy-Louis Vuitton (LVMH): The Rise of Talentism" written by Nancy Leung under the supervision of Frederic Godart and Andrew Shipilov.

Chalhoub's largest partners is Louis Vuitton Moët Hennessy (LVMH), with whom Chalhoub has several joint ventures, the oldest dating back to 1983. LVMH is a quintessential French-based luxury goods conglomerate that owns, among other businesses, such fashion brands as Berluti, Céline, and Kenzo; jewelry and watch brands such as TAG Heuer and Bulgari; and wine and spirits brands such as Moët & Chandon and Dom Pérignon.

Very often prospective partners approach Chalhoub with a proposed business model similar to the one Chalhoub uses in its alliance relationship with LVMH: the partner supplies its luxury products and Chalhoub sells these products in the Middle East. However, Chalhoub doesn't accept all proposals because the firm is very careful about building its alliance portfolio. The company's management recognizes that successful individual alliance relationships are the building blocks of network advantage. In other words, they have mastered the first-degree perspective. They have achieved first-degree network advantage. By getting these alliance relationships right, the Chalhoub Group gains greater second- and third-degree advantages as well.

How does the Chalhoub Group do this so successfully? Chalhoub uses the first-degree perspective and carefully selects partners that have the right "fit" with the firm. To guide you through the process of choosing individual alliance partners, we present the "Four Dimensions of Fit" framework. And we created the First-Degree Assessment Tool to help you evaluate complementarities and compatibilities in your existing alliance relationships. Let's begin by examining the first-degree perspective in detail.

Deciding which firms to form relationships with would be equivalent to the process used by Roman officials in ancient Britain to decide which new town they wanted to connect to Londinium by building a road. After building the road, the

Romans also had to periodically review its condition and repair as needed. Our First-Degree Assessment Tool can help you decide where to build your next alliance and how to repair existing relationships.

"Four Dimensions of Fit" Framework

A great deal has been written about ways to evaluate individual alliance relationships. Much of the research on this subject shows that the greater the compatibility and complementarity of a firm's partners, the higher is the probability of their alliance portfolio's success. To start the conversation about this topic in our executive education programs, we often use the "Four Dimensions of Fit" framework. This model suggests that to be successful companies need to form alliances with partners that provide a good "fit" in four dimensions—strategy, resources, organization, and culture.[2] Strategy and resource fit feed complementarity, and organization and culture fit support compatibility. This means that the most successful alliances occur between firms that have complementary strategies and resources as well as compatible organizations and cultures.

Let's look at the four dimensions individually. For each dimension, we provide a set of questions you can use to evaluate the fit between your firm and the proposed (or existing) alliance partner's firm. These same questions form the backbone of the First-Degree Assessment Tool which you can find in the Toolbox (see Appendix Two). Figure 3.1 summarizes the steps to follow in completing the First-Degree Assessment exercise.

Step 1: Evaluate Strategy Fit

Strategy fit implies the degree to which the partners have *complementary strategies*. This means that the collaboration should

---

[2]The original framework was suggested by Michael Yoshino.

Figure 3.1: Steps in the First-Degree Assessment

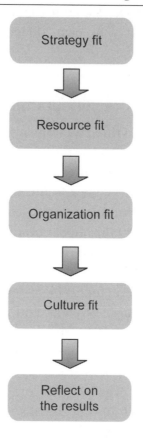

help both companies achieve their own long-term goals, but it should not make either firm a powerful competitor in the other firm's markets in the long run.

As an example, let's look at the relationship between Grundfos, the world's largest pump manufacturer based in Denmark, and Viessmann, the German-based maker of heating systems. If you're a European consumer and you have an advanced gas heater in your house, chances are it's made by Viessmann and it runs using a pump, sensor, or motor made by Grundfos. Because Grundfos specializes in making these components, it's very good at it. Viessmann specializes in the assembly of gas heaters using components from different suppliers like Grundfos. However, Grundfos is unlikely to start assembling gas heaters because its know-how is limited to making pumps and associated electronics. Viessmann is unlikely to start making advanced pumps because it lacks the know-how in that domain. Viessmann built strong brand recognition among consumers over time by making high-quality products and sponsoring major sporting events such as European skiing competitions. Therefore, Viessmann's capability in assembling the final product and its brand recognition are complementary to Grundfos's know-how about making essential parts of the final product. Both partners are unlikely to compete head to head in the future. All of these factors indicate good "strategy" fit.

Questions to Evaluate Strategy Fit

- What are the key objectives of this alliance from the standpoint of each partner?
- What are the key performance indicators for this alliance from the standpoint of both partners?
- What are each partner's long-term objectives?
- Are the partners current competitors or are they likely to compete in the same product or geographic markets in the future?
- How can this alliance help the partners achieve their competitive advantage?
- How might each partner cheat the other? What would each partner gain from each form of cheating?
- When will the partners exit the alliance? What are the exit terms?

You can evaluate strategy fit between your firm and its partners by asking the questions in the above box. The questions about performance objectives and exit terms are vitally important. Many alliances begin when senior executives from both companies meet at an industry event, "fall in love" with each other's strategic vision, and go home to tell their organizations that from now on they have an alliance. However, in order to help both companies clarify what they really want from the alliance as well as determine whether the other partner is serious about it, you need to determine the exit terms and key performance indicators in advance. During the "honeymoon" period before the relationship actually begins, if you and your partner cannot agree on how you will measure success of the relationship and discuss how the relationship should be terminated, there's a high probability that the relationship was not made in heaven.

Step 2: Evaluate Resource Fit

Resource fit has to do with complementarity between the resources the partners bring to the table. That is, an alliance makes sense when partners bring different resources to their relationship, for example, human, financial, technological, market access, knowledge, intellectual property, brand, or other resources. Here's a good example of resource fit. INSEAD has a very successful alliance relationship with Business Kolding (BK), an organization affiliated with the Chamber of Commerce in the Kolding area of Denmark. Business Kolding's mission is to increase the attractiveness of the Kolding region for innovation and investments. This alliance involves delivery of two executive education programs: Executive Management Program (EMP) and Executive Board Program (EBP). The EMP is a program for senior executives with a focus on providing participants with cutting-edge knowledge in strategy, innovation, and leadership, while the EBP is a program for board members to help them acquire better directorship skills. In the INSEAD–BK relationship, INSEAD provides the global brand, faculty, and educational facilities in Fontainebleau, France while BK markets the INSEAD programs in Scandinavia and delivers the first module of the program in Denmark. BK also helps INSEAD to increase its brand awareness in its market.

If your firm and its partners bring exactly the same resources to the table, this begs the question, why did you decide to collaborate in the first place? Unless both firms want to pool their similar resources to achieve economies of scale in some markets, it's best when partners contribute different resources to the relationship. This way both partners can gain from the alliance by creating synergies. You can evaluate resource fit between your firm and its partners by asking the following questions.

Questions to Evaluate Resource Fit

- What resources does each partner contribute to the relationship? Are they similar or different?
- How do the resources contributed by each partner increase the value of the resources provided by the other partner?
- What return on the contributed resources does each partner plan to obtain? How will each partner evaluate this return?
- How will each partner's resource contributions change over time?

Step 3: Evaluate Organization Fit

Organization fit requires that the partners have *compatible* organizational structures. In other words, they need to have formal management mechanisms that are not vastly different to the point that the companies cannot coordinate their decision making. For example, a highly hierarchical organization will find it easier to communicate and make decisions in an alliance with another highly hierarchical organization. The same hierarchical organization would find it more difficult to communicate and make decisions with a partner that has a flat, matrix-style organizational structure. Both INSEAD and BK have very flat organizations and the decision making on both sides is very quick, which greatly facilitates collaboration.

Private companies might have difficulties working with publicly-held firms because of the different time horizons over which their organizations make decisions. Not-for-profit firms will find it easier to work with other not-for-profit firms than with for-profit firms. Finally, if two firms have had prior collaborations, they are more likely to have developed collaborative routines that will facilitate their collaboration in the future. Use the following questions to evaluate the organization fit between your firm and its partners.

Questions to Evaluate Organization Fit

- What are the organizational structures of each firm? Are they similar or different?
- How quickly does each organization make decisions? How many layers of bureaucracy are involved in decision making?
- What is the ownership form of each partner? Are they similar or different?
- Have the partners collaborated in previous relationships? How successful were these relationships?

Step 4: Evaluate Culture Fit

Culture fit exists when the two companies have similar cultures which allow them to actually understand, appreciate, and work within each other's cultural values and belief systems. In other words, an alliance relationship works well when the organizational cultures are *compatible*. For example, a company with a culture focused on getting quick short-term results will find it difficult to collaborate with a company that places long-term value creation at the core of its culture. INSEAD and BK are both committed to building a long-term partnership based on win–win solutions for both parties. Both partners also share a passion for management education, which helps in delivering great programs. To evaluate the culture fit between your firm and your partner, use the following questions.

Questions to Evaluate Culture Fit

- What are the cultural values and belief systems of each partner? Are they similar or different?
- How does each partner handle conflict and uncertainty?
- What is each partner's attitude toward risk taking?
- How does each partner deal with new ideas?
- Are both partners looking for win–win solutions in alliances?
- Do both partners share the same national culture?

Step 5: Reflect on Results

After completing your evaluation of the four dimensions, the last step is perhaps the most important. Reflection encourages you to draw conclusions about your alliance with a particular partner and determine what next steps to take to strengthen or repair the relationship. For a potential alliance, your evaluation will help you make a decision about whether to pursue the opportunity.

Applying the "Four Dimensions of Fit" Framework: The Chalhoub Group Case

Now, let's go back to our discussion of collaborations between LVMH and the Chalhoub Group. These two companies enjoy a very successful relationship because they have strong complementarity in strategy and resources; they also have compatibility in organization and culture.

Strategy Fit

LVMH and Chalhoub have complementary strategies. The long-term vision of LVMH involves maintaining and expanding its position as the global provider of luxury goods with an increasing focus on emerging markets, including the Middle East. The long-term vision of Chalhoub involves selling luxury goods in the Middle East either directly or to retail stores that are not owned by the company. By and large, LVMH brands that work with Chalhoub don't need to build their own network of stores in the Middle East because Chalhoub handles retail and distribution. Chalhoub doesn't want to encroach on LVMH markets either, as it is not planning to diversify into producing luxury goods of its own. Thus, there is strategy fit between the two companies.

Resource Fit

This relationship also demonstrates resource fit because LVMH provides Chalhoub with high-quality luxury goods to sell as well as recognizable brands that, in many cases, took several decades, if not centuries, to build. Chalhoub provides market access and market intelligence. Each company contributes resources that the other partner doesn't have, so resource fit exists.

Organization Fit

Both companies have decentralized matrix organizational structures. Chalhoub is organized by different geographies and products while LVMH is also organized by products (brands) and geographies. Because of decentralization, the decision making is quick in both companies. Both companies are family owned[3] so they can focus on developing long-term business objectives, even when this sometimes conflicts with their short-term financial objectives. This indicates the presence of organization fit. Executives in both companies also find it easy to communicate with each other.

Culture Fit

Both companies enjoy a strong culture fit as well. First, family ownership of the companies means that the employees and the executives are encouraged to build long-term relationships. Second, both companies share deep attachment to the French culture. LVMH is a profoundly French company that has deep roots within the Parisian luxury industry. Chalhoub's family owners have francophone origins.

Capturing the "Four Dimensions of Fit": Alliance Fit Chart

We've created a useful chart called the Alliance Fit Chart, which you'll find in the Toolbox, to help you evaluate each of your firm's alliance relationships in terms of the Four Dimensions of Fit framework. Using this chart, you can evaluate each dimension of fit between you and your alliance partner (or potential partner) and assign a rating based on a simple five-point scale where:

1 = no fit at all
3 = some fit, but not great
5 = great fit

Table 3.1 shows a completed Alliance Fit Chart for the Chalhoub Group's relationship with LVMH. We've captured

---

[3] Despite the fact that LVMH is publicly traded, 42.2% of its shares are owned by Christian Dior, which in turn is 70% owned by Groupe Arnault, controlled by Bernard Arnault—the CEO and Board Chairman of LVMH. Chalhoub Group is owned by the Chalhoub family.

Table 3.1 Chalhoub's Alliance Fit Chart

Partner name	Strategy fit	Resource fit	Organization fit	Culture fit
LVMH	Partners share similar long-term visions Partners have different competitive strategies	Partners make different contributions to the relationship	Partners have similar formal management mechanisms	Partners have similar values and beliefs

Strategy fit	Resource fit	Organization fit	Culture fit
Chalhoub is a leading purveyor of luxury of products in the Middle East LVMH is a global manufacturer of luxury products with a growing focus on emerging markets LVMH does not compete with Chalhoub	Chalhoub provides market access and local knowledge LVMH provides luxury products with powerful brand recognition	Chalhoub and LVMH are decentralized organizations	Shared French cultural heritage Shared focus on building long-term relationships Family business values

Rating	5	5	5	5

Conclusion: relationship is to be continued and strengthened.

the rationale for each "fit" rating within each cell and then summarized the conclusions in the last column. In the Toolbox, you'll find an expanded version of this chart.

Using the First-Degree Assessment Tool

Now take a look at the First-Degree Assessment Tool in the Toolbox. If you notice that many of the questions sound a little legalistic, you're right. Alliances are like marriages, and marriages formed based only on love at first sight without any preparation often result in ruined expectations and acrimonious divorces. However, we don't intend to say that alliances should be negotiated by lawyers from day one. In fact, lawyers should be brought in only after the teams from both alliance partner firms have ironed out the general framework for cooperation including specific agreement about the:

- business model for the alliance
- resource contributions from each partner
- key performance indicators for the alliance
- exit date and exit terms

If your firm's lawyers are present from the first day of alliance negotiations, they will undermine the goodwill that you and your partner are slowly developing as you go through the process. At this initial stage, it's important to ask yourself two general questions:

- How valuable is the business opportunity created by the alliance complementarities?
- Is the compatibility between our organizations high enough to realize this value?

When using the First-Degree Assessment Tool, it's important to make sure your firm's executives openly discuss the merits of the proposed alliance along the Four Dimensions of Fit. If your discussion identifies major gaps between the strategy, resource, organization, or culture fit of your two companies and the gaps are too vast to overcome, then your company might be better off avoiding a relationship with that partner to begin with. If you're already in a relationship that scores poorly on some of the dimensions, then you either need to make an effort to improve these scores or terminate the relationship altogether.

First-Degree Assessment in Action: Philips Electronics

Philips Electronics, the Dutch multinational and one of the largest electronics firms in the world, has a formal process of ongoing alliance performance evaluation which is very similar to the Four Dimensions of Fit framework presented in this chapter. It uses three dimensions—strategic fit, cultural fit, and operational fit (a combination of resource and organization fit). Prior to formation of an alliance, Philips executives score the different potential partners on these dimensions. An executive who proposes a particular alliance has to persuade his colleagues that the alliance is a viable alternative to the other possible alliances or to accomplishing the task internally. The scoring process is not mechanical, so the system forces the executives to articulate what they really want from the alliance, how the partner is likely to deliver, and what the potential pitfalls are.

After Philips initiates an alliance, the alliance managers and executives from the business unit that "owns" the alliance periodically review its progress using a survey in which they are asked to evaluate different aspects of fit. They also ask executives from the partner companies to respond to the same survey. Because these are independent responses, they provide a treasure trove of information when they are compared. The higher the score both partners give on a particular sub-dimension, the better the alliance is at performing on that dimension. Big gaps in evaluation indicate problems the partners need to work together to resolve.

This kind of exercise serves as a great start for a company-wide initiative to evaluate your firm's entire alliance portfolio. If you have more than one alliance partner, use the First-Degree Assessment Tool to evaluate each individual relationship. If some relationships have low fit ratings, especially in the areas of strategy and resource fit, then you might decide to reallocate time and attention away from these relationships and toward other relationships in your portfolio. If the fit rating is high in terms of strategy and resource fit, but low on culture and organization fit, then this relationship warrants you paying more attention to the decision making across the partners and gaining better knowledge of each other's culture. Clearly, this exercise tells you what features of the relationship need attention.

Neglecting culture fit in any analysis can be dangerous and lead to unstable relationships. In 2003, British Petroleum (BP) formed a 50/50 joint venture, called the TNK–BP joint venture, with the Russian consortium Alfa-Access-Renova (AAR). In terms of resources, AAR contributed its holdings in TNK International, several Russian oil companies, and oil fields. BP contributed its own holdings in Russian oil companies and its BP Moscow retail network. Clear complementarities existed between the partners—BP provided its expertise in the energy sector while AAR provided BP with greater access to Russia's oil fields as well as political clout. However, the two parent companies had very different organizational cultures. Our conversations with people close to this joint venture suggest that AAR adopted a highly confrontational stance in dealing with BP, while the British partner was not ready for such confrontation. In its approach to negotiations, AAR adopted this philosophy: "You have to firmly hold your partner's [hand] with both hands and constantly increase the pressure." BP was also not used to being constantly pressured by its partners, which led to several major disputes and finally culminated in the termination of the TNK–BP joint venture. In late 2012, AAR sold its shares to Rosneft, a Russian state-oil giant, while BP swapped its 50% equity in TNK–BP for a 20% stake in Rosneft.[4]

What can you do to avoid a similar fate? Start each alliance partnership by using the First-Degree Assessment Tool to evaluate the presence of strategy, resource, organization, and culture fit.

Going Forward

Using the first-degree perspective to develop successful individual alliances gives your firm the fundamental building blocks for increasing your network advantage. These relationships establish your first-degree network advantage. You will not benefit from the second- or third-degree perspectives unless you have chosen compatible and complementary partners. Now, assuming you have achieved strategic, resource, organization, and culture fit with your partners, let's discuss how you can obtain second-degree network advantage—generating greater information, cooperation, and power from your alliance portfolio.

Chapter Highlights

- Understanding the first degree of your network advantage requires thinking about whether areas of complementarity or compatibility exist between you and your partners.

---

[4] http://online.wsj.com/article/SB1000142412788732402400045781730
10700848822.html.

- At the first-degree perspective, using the Four Dimensions of Fit framework allows you to assess the strategy, resource, organization, and culture fit between you and your partners. Strategy and resource fit promote finding complementarities; organization and culture fit support establishing compatibilities.
- To assess the degree of fit for each dimension, use the First-Degree Assessment Tool. The results will help you make decisions to start new alliances or take action on repairing or terminating existing alliances.
- The First-Degree Assessment Tool serves as a basis for robust discussion internally and for structuring win–win discussions with potential and current partners.

CHAPTER FOUR

THE SECOND-DEGREE PERSPECTIVE: UNDERSTANDING THE ALLIANCE PORTFOLIO CONFIGURATIONS THAT DELIVER NETWORK ADVANTAGE

When the devastating earthquake and tsunami struck Japan on March 11, 2011, the production facilities of Renesas Electronics in Naka town were hit hard. This major producer of microchips for the auto industry relies on "clean rooms" with completely sterile and dust-free conditions, but the earthquake cracked walls and ceilings, filled the building with dust and debris, and caused its production equipment to lose alignment. Thankfully, Renesas Electronics had strong alliances with its customers—the automakers. Even though its customers had intense rivalries and were in an industry that has traditionally thrived on pitting weak suppliers against each other, Renesas had a very high share of the market for intelligent chips used in cars. The earthquake created an instant crisis for the automobile industry because the production stoppage at Renesas could have halted production of cars across the board.

What happened next shows what alliance networks can do for a firm when a crisis hits. Renesas's customers and suppliers responded promptly by sending up to 2,500 of their own workers to the Naka plant. In Singapore and Taiwan, the firm's contract foundries accelerated their pace of production to fill some of the gap during the production stoppage. By mobilizing the network, Renesas limited production slowdowns and stoppages among automakers to just a few weeks, and its Naka plant was back to full production in September, one month ahead of schedule.[1]

To accomplish this feat, Renesas tapped into and coordinated the efforts of many alliance partners rather than working with its partners individually. In other words, its second-degree network advantage saved the day. Recall how Londinium's commerce thrived not only because of the individual highways leading to the city but also because of the broader network of highways that connected Londinium's neighbors to each other. Likewise, Renesas's alliance portfolio configuration contained the interconnections that helped the firm recover rapidly from the natural disaster.

So let's expand the field of vision and focus on using the second-degree perspective to increase your firm's access to information, cooperation, and power. Your firm can generate different kinds of second-degree network advantage by choosing different alliance portfolio configurations. To help you determine which of the three possible configurations of alliance portfolios—hub-and-spoke, integrated, or hybrid—will deliver sustained second-degree advantage for your firm, we've developed a framework called the Configuration Alignment Tool

---

[1]Courtland, R. 2011. How Japanese chipmaker Renesas recovered from the earthquake. *IEEE Spectrum*, August.

Figure 4.1: A generic hub-and-spoke alliance portfolio

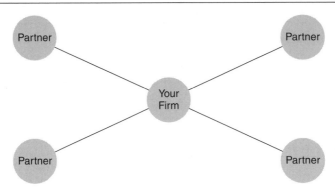

(CAT). You'll learn the concepts underlying the CAT in this chapter and then how to use the CAT in the following chapter.

Hub-and-Spoke Alliance Portfolio Configuration

The hub-and-spoke alliance portfolio configuration features disconnected partners. Each tie in this portfolio is called an *open tie*. An open tie means the central firm's partners are not connected to one another. Figure 4.1 represents an example of a hub-and-spoke alliance portfolio. From the center firm's position all of the ties in this network are open.

Now look at Figure 4.2, which illustrates the alliance portfolios for Pfizer and Biocon. This picture shows that all of Pfizer's and Biocon's ties are open because none of their partners have connections or ties to each other. Pfizer and Biocon are positioned at the "hubs" of these ties.

By building a hub-and-spoke alliance portfolio, a firm can capitalize on combining the unique differences between its partners and generate second-degree network advantage as follows:

- The *information advantage* comes from the fact that the hub firm aggregates private knowledge from its disconnected

Figure 4.2: Hub-and-spoke alliance portfolios of Pfizer and Biocon

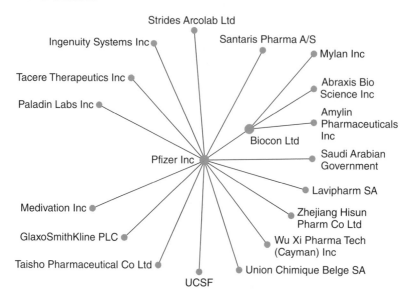

spokes. Each "spoke" partner doesn't know what the other partners know. Only firms at the hubs of open ties, like Pfizer and Biocon, are able to integrate the information flowing from these disconnected ties.

- The *cooperation advantage* comes from the firm's ability to enforce partners' cooperativeness through bilateral agreements.
- The *power advantage* comes from the firm's ability to put partners in competition for its attention or resources. The "hub" firm can capitalize on the absence of ties between its partners by either playing them against each other or using the learnings from one partner in its dealings with another partner. Pfizer's partners, for example, rely on it more than Pfizer relies on any one of them to access the broader

network. Only Biocon has ties to partners other than Pfizer, which partially mitigates Pfizer's power advantage.

There are disadvantages to being at the center of a hub-and-spoke portfolio:

- *Isolation.* It can be rather lonely. If something goes wrong with Pfizer or Biocon, for instance, they can expect little help from their alliance partners.
- *Competitiveness.* Research clearly shows that hub-and-spoke portfolios induce competitiveness between partners. On average, open ties are also more difficult to maintain over long periods of time. These partners are less likely to work together to collectively fix Pfizer's or Biocon's problems.
- *Lack of trust.* Open-tie partners have difficulty fully trusting the hub firm because they know that they can be played off each other at any point in time. They also have difficulty trusting each other because they might be competing against each other—in fact, they may have already had that experience.

Integrated Alliance Portfolio Configuration

As an alternative to the hub-and-spoke alliance portfolio, the integrated portfolio configuration features interconnections between all of the firm's partners. Individual ties in this portfolio are called *closed ties*, which means that they connect partners who are also connected to each other. Figure 4.3 shows a generic integrated portfolio configuration.

Many airlines have integrated portfolios because of their membership in one of the large airline alliances. Let's take a look at Continental Airlines, a major U.S. carrier, which belonged to the Star Alliance. This company had codeshare agreements and shared frequent flyer programs, lounge access, and information infrastructure with other Star Alliance members

Figure 4.3: A generic integrated alliance portfolio

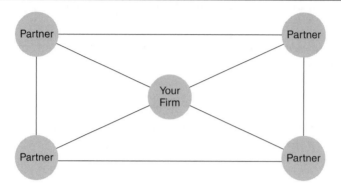

Figure 4.4: Integrated alliance portfolio of
Continental Airlines

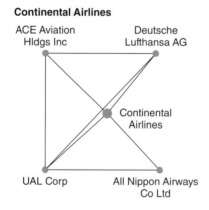

such as United Airlines, Air Canada (which is owned by the ACE Aviation Holdings), Lufthansa, and All Nippon Airways. As shown in Figure 4.4, an integrated alliance portfolio configuration helped Continental to develop economies of scale with trusted partners, and its relationship with United Airlines worked so well the two eventually merged.

Integrated portfolios don't always lead to mergers between partners, but they do help secure cooperation and develop trust. Renesas was an extreme example, but even firms that are not in crisis can benefit from having an integrated network. This portfolio configuration capitalizes on the interconnections between partners and delivers second-degree network advantage as follows:

- The *information advantage* comes from the ability of all firms to share common knowledge. There is no single firm that aggregates the knowledge, and what is known to one partner quickly becomes known to all others.
- The *cooperation advantage* comes from the ability of the portfolio group as a whole to ensure the good conduct of its individual partners. One partner cannot cheat another partner without spoiling its relationships with the other common partners. If this happens, the partners can work together to repair the relationship between the two partners or they can group together to collectively penalize the firm that misbehaved. For example, if Continental decides to "cheat" Air Canada in some collaborative effort, all the other partners will know about this. If one partner decides to help another, it doesn't need to do this on its own. Just like in the Renesas example, partners in an integrated portfolio can collectively provide a helping hand.
- The *power advantage* comes from the firms' ability to mobilize collective resources to fight common enemies. The integrated portfolio of Continental Airlines, for instance, helps all partner firms to achieve economies of scale by optimizing their route networks, making joint purchasing decisions for equipment, sharing loyalty programs, and competing against other large airline alliances.

There are some disadvantages to the integrated portfolio configuration:

- *Reduced potential for radical innovation.* Integrated portfolios don't help companies make the kinds of radical innovations that come from adding up disparate knowledge in fundamentally new ways.

- *Difficulty terminating.* This configuration might even force a firm to get stuck with alliances that have outlived their usefulness. For example, one partner might have been a great fit 10 years ago, but now the world has moved on and the partner can no longer deliver. In the hub-and-spoke network, the hub firm can terminate cooperation with this partner at any time. The other partners have nothing to say about it because they are not connected to the dropped "spoke" partner. In an integrated portfolio, when a firm ends an alliance, the other partners connected to the terminated partner will see what happened and start worrying about their own alliances with that partner.

- *Costly impact of termination.* The concern about how other partners will react to terminating a partner could be enough to make a firm consider keeping that partner after all. A firm's reputation has value, and losing the firm's reputation for being a dependable partner can be especially costly in an integrated portfolio.

Hybrid Alliance Portfolio Configuration

As you may have guessed by now, the hybrid alliance portfolio is a combination of the integrated and hub-and-spoke portfolio configurations. A hybrid alliance portfolio has some open ties and some closed ties. In other words, some partners in a hybrid network are connected to each other, while other partners are not. Figure 4.5 presents an example of this portfolio configuration.

As depicted in Figure 4.6, Lufthansa has a hybrid alliance portfolio.

The left-hand side of this picture is to be expected for an airline; it shows Lufthansa's interconnections with the Star Alliance members:

Figure 4.5: A generic hybrid alliance portfolio

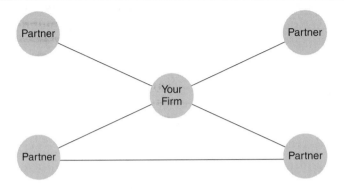

Figure 4.6: Hybrid alliance portfolio of Lufthansa

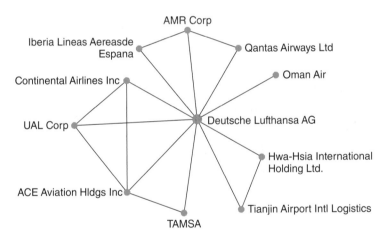

- Air Canada (ACE Aviation Hldgs. Inc.)
- Continental Airlines
- United (UAL Corp.)
- TAMSA

We saw most of these relationships in the Continental Airlines alliance portfolio picture (Figure 4.4). Lufthansa also formed relationships with three other partners which are more interesting relationships because these partners are members of Oneworld—an alliance network that competes with Star Alliance:

- Qantas
- Iberia
- American Airlines (AMR Corp.)

Lufthansa, Qantas, Iberia, and American Airlines formed a four-partner alliance in August 2008 to cooperate commercially on flights between the United States, Mexico, Canada, Switzerland, Norway, and the European Union; in July 2007 these partners also formed an alliance to provide aviation marketing services. This alliance with the "enemies" seemed to run completely against the principles of Star Alliance. Yet, Lufthansa participated in this alliance not directly but through its ownership of British Midland International (BMI) airline.[2] Although Lufthansa eventually sold BMI in 2012, for close to 10 years it was able to keep a foothold in two global airline alliances.

Lufthansa's alliance with Qantas is also interesting because the relationship is deeper than many airline alliances. These two companies formed a joint venture called Jet Turbine Services to provide commercial aircraft engine maintenance, repair, and overhaul services in Australia.[3]

In addition to these two parts of its portfolio, Lufthansa has alliances with the three partners shown in Table 4.1.

As you can see, these pictures tell a story of the strategy Lufthansa uses to generate footholds in the global air transport markets. On the one hand, it relies on using the benefits of

---

[2] http://en.wikipedia.org/wiki/British_Midland_International.
[3] http://www.ltq.com.au/LTQAbout%20Us.html.

Table 4.1 Lufthansa's alternative alliance portfolio

Partner	Alliance objective
Oman Air	Offer aircraft maintenance for the Airbus A330, Boeing 737 NG, ATR 42 belonging to Oman Air and its other customers[4]
Hwa-Hsia International Holding Ltd	Provide air freight services in China[5]
Tianjin Airport International Logistics	Provide air freight services in China[6]

collaboration and trust from its Star Alliance partners to collectively exploit opportunities in Europe and North America. Unlike the weaker Continental Airlines, Lufthansa retained its bargaining power over the Star Alliance partners by using collaboration with members of the Oneworld alliance to access the same markets. On the other hand, through its alliance with Oman Air, Lufthansa explores new revenue opportunities by providing maintenance services for its own aircraft and the aircraft of its partners (such as United Airlines and American) in Australia and the Middle East. Finally, through the alliance with Hwa-Hsia International Holding Ltd. and Tianjin Airport International Logistics, Lufthansa is well positioned to benefit from the growing air freight services in Asia as well as from the projected increase in traffic flow between the United States and Asia. No single partner is unique in Lufthansa's network;

---

[4] http://www.omanair.com/wy/aboutus/media/press-releases/oman-air-inks-strategic-deal-lufthansa-technik.

[5] http://www.german-company-directory.com.

[6] http://www.german-company-directory.com/?menuaction=contactmgr.ui.view&id=7544.

it can easily replace its reliance on one partner in one market with reliance on a different partner.

As the Lufthansa example shows, the second-degree network advantages of the hybrid alliance portfolio configuration are a combination of the advantages of the integrated and hub-and-spoke portfolio configurations:

- The *information advantage* comes from the ability to both integrate the knowledge across unconnected partners and share common knowledge across connected partners.
- The *cooperation advantage* comes from the firm's ability to both secure bilateral cooperation of unconnected partners and benefit from the joint cooperation of connected partners.
- The *power advantage* comes from the firm's ability to both play off unconnected partners against each other and use the connected partners to quickly mobilize resources against common threats.

In terms of disadvantages, the hybrid portfolio configuration involves these challenges:

- *Less trust.* The hybrid configuration generates a lower level of trust between partners, especially when compared to the integrated portfolio. While some partners might join forces to come and help another partner in times of need, other partners will not.
- *Fewer breakthrough innovations.* Hybrid portfolios are likely to produce fewer breakthrough innovations than a hub-and-spoke portfolio.
- *Difficulty managing.* A firm has to manage the hybrid portfolio in two different ways. The knowledge and activities a firm needs to get the greatest value from the hub-and-spoke part of its portfolio differ from what the firm needs to get

the greatest value from the integrated part of its portfolio. For example, the search for new opportunities in the hub-and-spoke portion is different from the search for refinement and improvement opportunities in the integrated portion. Because the hybrid structure combines these two very different portfolio configurations, firms could find it difficult to manage.

Renesas's Hybrid Portfolio Configuration: A Blend of the Two

Now let's look at the picture of the alliance portfolio for Renesas Electronics. Since this firm is a "daughter" company of NEC Corp. and Hitachi Corp., which collectively own over 64% of its shares,[7] we aggregated NEC's and Hitachi's alliances into Figure 4.7.

As many of Renesas's partners are connected, but others are not, the firm has a hybrid portfolio. The closed ties in its portfolio are with the partners who came to its aid after the 2011 earthquake disaster.

The partners that Renesas had open ties with were less likely to come to its aid, but they are the ones that provide Renesas with opportunities to create breakthrough innovations. Open ties help Renesas to access knowledge from different industries. Its alliance with Nokia involves transfer to Renesas of Nokia's knowledge in fourth-generation mobile cellular communication while its joint venture with Sharp and Powerchip Semiconductors involves the manufacturing, design, and sales of LCD drivers and controllers for small-size LCD panels. So, the hybrid portfolio allows Renesas to both integrate the differences between the partners and secure their cooperation in the event of emergency.

---

[7] http://en.wikipedia.org/wiki/Renesas_Electronics.

Figure 4.7: Hybrid alliance portfolio of Renesas Electronics

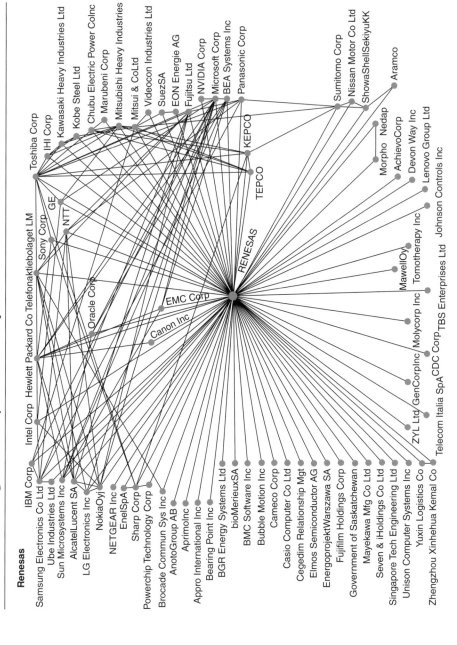

The Configuration Alignment Tool (CAT): Conceptual Overview

Over the past 20 years, most of our research on the second-degree perspective has focused on analyzing the conditions under which a firm should build a particular type of alliance portfolio configuration: hub-and-spoke, integrated, or hybrid. The Configuration Alignment Tool (CAT) is based on this research and it helps you to analyze your firm based on three key factors:

- industry dynamism
- breadth of product or service range
- market power

What follows is a conceptual overview of these factors. In Chapter 5, we explain how to use the CAT factors to assess your firm's alliance portfolio configuration.

Industry Dynamism

Industries are considered dynamic if they often experience sudden and unpredictable changes in technology, demand, competition, or any other important feature of the industry. If these changes are infrequent, then the industry is considered stable. Companies in more dynamic industries thrive with hub-and-spoke portfolios while companies in stable industries benefit from integrated portfolios. In one study, we discovered that in stable industries such as steel-making, firms with integrated portfolios had higher returns on assets as compared to firms with hub-and-spoke portfolios. We found a different situation in dynamic industries, such as semiconductors, where firms with more hub-and-spoke portfolios had higher returns on assets as compared to firms with integrated portfolios.[8]

---

[8] Rowley, T., D. Behrens, and D. Krackhardt. 2000. Redundant governance structures: An analysis of structural and relational embeddedness in the steel and semiconductor industries. *Strategic Management Journal* 21: 369–386.

The airline industry is much less dynamic than the pharmaceutical or semiconductor industries; disruptive innovations are less likely among the airlines than in these other two fields. In a dynamic industry that experiences rapid changes, an integrated alliance portfolio can become a liability because it constrains the firm to the particular pool of knowledge available to its immediate circle of partners and doesn't allow for reaching out. Hub-and-spoke portfolios help firms collect information and connect to opportunities quickly. They are more suitable for firms operating in industries that see a constant flow of new opportunities that are difficult for a single firm to monitor and exploit. In these situations, the hub-and-spoke portfolio is superior because every tie is a potential source of unique new information.

A hub-and-spoke alliance portfolio is also beneficial in a dynamic industry because it provides partners with flexibility in forming new ties or dropping old ones. In other words, the partners are willing to stop collaboration if the window for exploiting an opportunity passes before they are able to make full use of it. Unlike the integrated portfolios found in more static industries, hub-and-spoke portfolios allow firms in dynamic industries to initiate and dissolve ties depending on the arrival and departure of opportunities. And breaking ties is not seen as a signal that a firm is a bad collaborator. Often in stable industries, breaking a tie does not mean that conditions have changed; it means that something went wrong in the alliance.

Take, for example, Biocon, the firm whose alliance portfolio we pictured in Figure 4.2. This Indian biotech firm, founded in 1978 and with 2012 revenues of $446 million, initially made enzymes used in food production through a proprietary fermentation process and then expanded into biopharmaceuticals in 1995. The firm is now producing high-value pharmaceuticals such as statins (used to control cholesterol level). Its expansion was made possible in part through strategic alliances. In October 2010, Biocon and Pfizer established an alliance designed to allow Pfizer to sell insulin products manufactured by Biocon, but they canceled the joint venture in March 2012. Both companies indicated that the joint venture had become unviable due to their different strategic priorities.[9] Pfizer paid Biocon for the cancellation.

As we might expect for firms operating in this very dynamic industry, neither firm has taken a big hit to its reputation as a result of the joint venture blow up. This would not have been the case in an integrated alliance portfolio because the termination of a relationship that is surrounded by relationships with other partners is usually much more public and damaging to reputations. Thus, firms in integrated portfolios are tempted to keep their existing relationships alive, even though the world may have moved on and the existing relationships can no longer provide value. As another incentive to maintain a less satisfactory alliance, consider this example. If a major airline exits a particular alliance, its shares as well as the shares of the other alliance members are likely to suffer much more than a pharmaceutical industry firm in similar circumstances. Financial markets expect more stability in the airline industry than in pharmaceuticals.

Breadth of Product or Service Range

The next factor involves the simple relationship between the breadth of a firm's product range and the alliance portfolio needed to support it. The narrower the range of a company's products or services, the more the company will benefit from an integrated alliance portfolio. The wider the range of the company's products or services, the more likely the company will benefit from a hub-and-spoke alliance portfolio.

---

[9] http://en.tengrinews.kz/companies/8380/.

To succeed with a hub-and-spoke portfolio, a firm needs to be able to deal with diversity of ideas, processes, and resources. A company with a broad product or service range already has the necessary internal capabilities to deal with all three kinds of diversity. For example, it has people with different professional backgrounds who collectively see more opportunities resulting from recombining ideas and insights from different partners in the hub-and-spoke portfolio. Companies that have a broad product range based on different geographies (i.e. selling products in different countries) employ individuals from different countries or individuals who have cross-cultural professional experiences. These people are likely to be more at ease with connecting previously unconnected ideas, concepts, or solutions learned from alliance partners to new products or services that the "hub" firm can provide. If the company knows how to deal with diversity internally, it can also benefit from external diversity. In contrast, a highly specialized company (e.g., selling a single type of product in a single geographical location) in a hub-and-spoke alliance portfolio will not have the necessary ability to deal with outside diversity.

To test this diversity argument, we studied investment banks in Canada to determine whether their membership in syndicates formed to underwrite Initial Public Offerings (IPOs) in the financial markets would have an impact on their market share. We found that investment banks that underwrote public offerings for firms in a variety of industries had higher market share when they had hub-and-spoke alliance portfolios. Diverse experiences from underwriting IPOs in different industries helped these banks to better absorb the diverse information received from unconnected partners. In contrast, investment banks that underwrote IPOs in a small number of industries performed better when their alliance portfolios were more integrated.[10]

---

[10] Shipilov, A.V. 2006. Network strategies and performance of Canadian investment banks. *Academy of Management Journal* 49(3): 590–604.

Likewise, in a different study, we found that partnerships between investment banks doing business in the United Kingdom had a higher share of the market for mergers and acquisitions (M&A) advice if they had hub-and-spoke alliance portfolios and had experience advising clients from different industries and countries.[11]

Intel provides a practical example of the effect of product range breadth on choosing the optimal alliance portfolio configuration. Intel is a much more diversified company than Renesas. As you know, Intel makes a broad range of products:

- microprocessors
- motherboard chipsets
- network interface controllers
- flash memory chips
- graphic chips
- embedded processors
- other devices related to applications in computing, data security, data storage, retail networking, and communications

In contrast, Renesas focuses specifically on designing and manufacturing microcontrollers (a type of microchip) primarily for the automotive industry and mobile phones. That's a much narrower range of products.

As a collective unit, Intel's executives have diverse backgrounds and work experience in each of its different product lines. Like many other Japanese firms, Renesas tends to promote only Japanese executives to its senior leadership positions. As a result, it lacks some of the internal diversity that results from building senior management teams with different national

---

[11]Shipilov, A.V. 2009. Firm scope experience, historic multimarket contact with partners, centrality, and the relationship between structural holes and performance. *Organization Science* 20(1): 85–106.

backgrounds.[12] These pieces add up to Intel being better able to "absorb" diverse ideas and insights from its partners than Renesas, so Intel benefits more from its hub-and-spoke portfolio.

It may appear that diverse firms can make better use of any portfolio configuration, not only the hub-and-spoke configuration. Actually, diverse firms can't use integrated portfolios as well as specialized firms. An integrated alliance portfolio involves firms that co-specialize; that is, they specialize in producing different parts or delivering different services that complement each other. If a company specializes in making one part of a product or service, this company may make its part much cheaper and more efficiently than a company that makes several different parts for the same product or service. However, this company that specializes is also vulnerable to the behavior of other partners because its part is worthless without the parts made by the other portfolio partners.

In the automotive industry, suppliers to Toyota or other manufacturers make parts of the bigger product—a car—and if one partner fails to produce a quality part, then the final product cannot be made. Information exchange and informal coordination in the integrated alliance portfolio help make sure that every partner works toward the common goal and will make its parts available to the other partners when needed. The coordination in a good integrated network is so close that it is almost as if the alliance managers on each side are members of the same firm. But in order for that to go smoothly, they can't be forced to compete for the attention of top management against managers of different product lines. The integrated network portfolio calls for full commitment

---

[12] Black, S. and Morrison, A.J. 2010. *Sunset in the Land of the Rising Sun: Why Japanese Multinational Corporations Will Struggle in the Global Future*. INSEAD Business Press.

among partners; it's hard for any business unit of a diverse firm to commit fully.

Market Power

A firm can extract maximum advantage from a hub-and-spoke alliance portfolio when it has a lot of market power. Firms with less market power find integrated portfolios more beneficial. Integrated networks give firms an opportunity to fight a common enemy, be it a natural disaster or powerful competitors. Nowhere is this dynamic more apparent than in the auto industry. Over the past 40 years, the Japanese automakers have been smaller than the Big Three U.S. automakers. Given the technological and market advances that automakers face, this difference in size translated into a disadvantage in product development and procurement for the Japanese, which needed to be counteracted through better organization. Collaboration within integrated alliance networks enabled Japanese car makers to develop a critical mass to take on the U.S. market. Once they fine-tuned the close coordination approach, it worked so well that the Japanese automakers could redesign models faster than their U.S. counterparts even with smaller in-house design units.

Market power is not just seen in the higher prices a firm gets for its products. It also gives a firm greater ability to bargain for equipment and supplies, and often it even allows a firm to attract the highest quality employees at lower prices than its competitors. Because of its brand, Intel can clearly charge higher prices for its products. Intel also has significant internal resources (including spare capacity, cash, and human capital) that it gets at prices which allow Intel the flexibility to compete at even lower prices than those it currently charges. These resources also allow Intel to weather a crisis without needing support from partners in an integrated portfolio. If a crisis erupts, the firm can reallocate resources to different uses.

Intel doesn't need its partners to staff its factories in the event of a disaster; it can do so by itself.

Powerful firms also have the ability to create hub-and-spoke networks, possibly against the wishes of their alliance partners. Intel has enough power (and access to proprietary technology) to prevent its partners from working together and eventually bypassing Intel. For example, in 2008 Intel and Comcast formed a strategic alliance to develop widget channel framework web-based software in the United States.[13] In computing, a widget is a piece of hardware that brings Internet-driven interactive features to televisions by exploiting simple software components.[14] This alliance is expected to combine Internet-based applications with a television through a widget-based user interface that can be easily accessed while watching television programs. At the same time, Intel and Yahoo also announced an alliance to work on widgets in the United States.[15] Clearly, Intel is learning something from each alliance partner that it can then use in its relationships with other partners. However, even if Comcast and Yahoo might benefit from directly collaborating on the development of widget technology and bypass Intel, they would be unlikely to do so because they would be afraid of upsetting a powerful partner, which also happens to produce the hardware that both Comcast and Yahoo need to produce the widgets. This lets Intel place itself as the hub between these two spokes.

Having the power to force other firms to be a spoke in one's alliance portfolio is an important factor. Alliances between

---

[13] http://www.popularmechanics.com/technology/gadgets/news/4279779.

[14] http://www.cedmagazine.com/news/2011/06/details-emerge-on-comcast%27s-xcalibur%3B-roberts-demo-to-follow.

[15] http://www.reuters.com/article/2008/08/20/us-intel-yahoo-tv-idUSN2046725020080820.

companies are different from roads linking cities. Whereas significant distances could have made it impractical for some of the towns connected to Roman Londinium to have a direct road connection, alliances don't really involve distances. It's safe to assume that all firms in an industry will jockey for competitive advantage, and that sometimes means trying to avoid being a spoke. In a world without clear distances between companies and no provincial officials to dictate which connections are worth investing in, a firm has to rely on its own power to shape the alliance network.

Putting the Factors Together

Based on these three factors—industry dynamism, product breadth, and market power—use the CAT to compare your firm's current alliance portfolio configuration with the optimal configuration predicted by the tool. For each factor, assign a rating (high, medium, or low) for your firm. Based on where these ratings fall on the grid, the CAT determines your firm's optimal portfolio configuration. Using Renesas, Intel, and Continental as examples, Figure 4.8 summarizes the results of evaluating each firm based on the three factors. It shows that the actual portfolio configurations of Renesas, Intel, and Continental match the optimal configurations predicted by using the CAT.

For Renesas, the hybrid portfolio is best because it competes in an industry with moderate dynamism, it has neither a highly specialized nor highly diversified product range, and it has average market power. A hybrid configuration is also appropriate when different factors in the tool point to different options. For example, a hybrid portfolio would be advantageous for a specialized and low market power firm which competes in a highly dynamic industry. Conversely, a highly diversified firm with high market power that competes in a stable industry will also benefit from a hybrid portfolio.

Figure 4.8: The Configuration Alignment Tool
(Continental, Renesas, Intel)

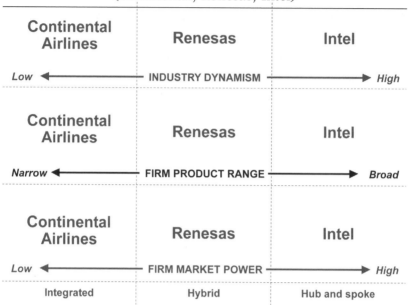

Intel needs (and can afford to) have a hub-and-spoke alliance portfolio because it competes in a highly dynamic industry, it has a wide product range, and it commands high market power.

Continental correctly chose to build an integrated portfolio. Its business largely focused on the United States so it was geographically specialized. The airline industry is stable because it is not subject to new and radically different technologies or ways of transporting people. Innovation in this industry is largely incremental. This firm also had relatively low market power as compared to the larger firms such as Lufthansa, Delta Airlines, and Air France-KLM. These factors place Continental to the left on the CAT grid. Many firms in the automotive industry or shipping industry would also belong on the left-hand side of the CAT grid.

Figure 4.9: The Configuration Alignment Tool (Sony)

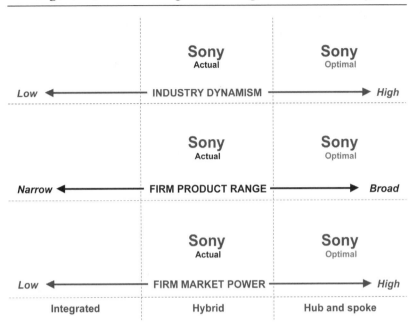

This tool can also help explain why Sony's hybrid alliance portfolio configuration, which we discussed in Chapter 2, was not optimal for Sony's industry and strategy. Sony's optimal versus actual portfolio configurations are shown in Figure 4.9.

Sony was competing in a highly dynamic industry. The firm had a wide product range and high market power. These factors should have allowed Sony to build a successful hub-and-spoke alliance portfolio. This is what is indicated on the right-hand side of the CAT picture.

Instead, Sony built a hybrid alliance portfolio which connected Sony to more limited pools of new information, knowledge, and resources than were optimal for its industry and strategy. Thus, Sony's alliance portfolio suffocated the company. In contrast, Samsung's alliance portfolio, which focused on producing hardware, was much more hub-and-spoke and allowed it to successfully compete within a dynamic industry, take advantage of its broad product portfolio, and utilize the company's high market power.

Going Forward

In the next chapter, we'll show how you can visualize your company's alliance portfolio and determine whether you have the right alliance portfolio structure to unlock the highest levels of second-degree network advantage.

Chapter Highlights

- Hub-and-spoke, integrated, and hybrid alliance portfolios each deliver their own unique sources of second-degree network advantage in terms of information, cooperation, and power.
- Making the choice between a hub-and-spoke, integrated, or hybrid portfolio configuration depends on three factors: industry dynamism, the company's breadth of product offerings, and the company's market power.
- Hub-and-spoke portfolios work best when a company is in a highly dynamic industry, has a broad product or service range, and has a lot of market power.
- Integrated portfolios work best when a company is in a stable industry, has a narrow product or service range, and has low market power.

CHAPTER FIVE

EVALUATING AND CHANGING YOUR ALLIANCE PORTFOLIO CONFIGURATION

Rabobank, a multinational financial services company based in the Netherlands, plays an active role in food and agribusiness financing. Its development unit, Rabo Development, provides developing societies with better access to financial services, improves the food and agribusiness market, and employs cooperative principles as well as its banking expertise. The Rabo Development business model involves building alliances with banks in developing countries such as Zambia, Tanzania, Rwanda, Mozambique, Uganda, Paraguay, Brazil, and China, and through these alliances it supports financial institutions with technical assistance upon request. It deepens its alliances by taking a minority stake in the partner, offering management support for key positions, or providing technical assistance on specific assignments. The partner pays management fees for these services.

Partners gain an important benefit by becoming part of Rabobank's knowledge network and alliance portfolio. To allow its partners to learn from each other, Rabo Development organizes annual conferences at which its directors and its partners' CEOs share knowledge on market trends, change management, and ways to solve common problems. Meetings at these conferences also allow partners to establish direct alliances, which have led to the development of new integrated financial service products for major clients involved in international business transactions.

You can see that these conferences help Rabobank to build an integrated network portfolio. As the partners learn from one another, their performance improves and Rabobank's knowledge base in developing countries improves as well. Unlike its competitors from Western Europe and the United States, Rabobank has built a robust network of alliances that resembles a dense highway system of connections which provide benefits to all members. The network facilitates the flow of information, cooperation, and power across national borders, helping these countries to develop established financial systems. It delivers second-degree network advantage.

Does this example and the others you've seen so far inspire you to think about which portfolio configuration *your* firm should have to reap second-degree network advantage? If so, you're already escaping the first-degree myopia that holds so many companies back. This chapter contains several tools that will help you think about the configuration of your firm's alliance portfolio. While the First-Degree Assessment Tool introduced in Chapter 3 helps you think about your firm's individual relationships, the Second-Degree Assessment Tool introduced in this chapter helps you visualize your firm's overall alliance portfolio from the second-degree perspective. Using the Configuration Alignment Tool (CAT) introduced in Chapter 4, you'll also learn strategies for changing the configuration of your alliance portfolio if the CAT indicates that you could achieve greater network advantage with a different configuration of your alliance portfolio.

Visualizing the Second Degree

We've already used alliance pictures to illustrate hub-and-spoke, integrated, and hybrid portfolios. When there are not too many firms in the portfolio, these pictures are easy to understand, just as the map of Roman Britannia (Figure I.1) was easy to read. These pictures give you a simple visual aid for understanding alliance portfolios and can help you in planning changes to them. Because it is so important that you "see" your portfolio at one glance, this section has more techniques to help you visualize your alliance portfolio and act on the analysis.

Simplified Alliance Portfolios

In previous chapters you saw first-degree pictures showing all the alliances of a firm on one page. The pictures basically looked like spider webs of alliance partners. When the connections between alliance partners are included, these second-degree pictures become highly informative because they show whether the network surrounding a firm is integrated or hub-and-spoke. Recall that once those lines were added, the differences between the alliance portfolios of Samsung and Sony became obvious (see Chapter 2). The lines also helped show the alliance portfolios in the stories of Lufthansa and Continental (see Chapter 4).

For a different, simplified way to capture the second-degree perspective of a company's portfolio, look at Figure 5.1. This picture of Chalhoub Group's alliance portfolio shows that Chalhoub has relationships with suppliers beyond LVMH, the company discussed in Chapter 3. In fact it has a strong relationship with Puig, a Spanish fashion conglomerate which also happens to be family-owned, has a strong preference for building long-term relationships with its partners, and seeks opportunities to grow in emerging markets.

Figure 5.1: Simplified picture of Chalhoub's alliance portfolio

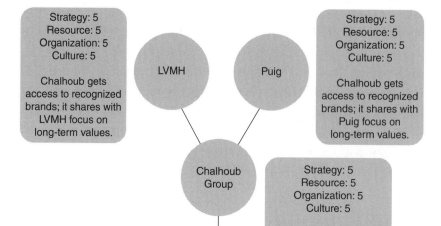

Figure 5.1 shows a simplified view of Chalhoub's portfolio because, in reality, Chalhoub has more suppliers, and it also sells through different retailers whose strategy, resource, organization, and culture fit need to be evaluated separately. What is common across these retailers, however, is that they provide Chalhoub with market knowledge and local contacts that it can use to help to sell the products of LVMH and Puig in the Middle East. This picture shows that Chalhoub is acting as a "luxury bridge to the Middle East." It is not a coincidence that the company's website also refers to Chalhoub as the "bridge" between Eastern and Western cultures.

Being a bridge essentially means that a company is at the center of its hub-and-spoke network. Just like Londinium acted as a bridge between Dover and Chichester, Chalhoub is a bridge between Puig and LVMH. Knowledge travels across alliances like goods across the highways. By being a "bridge" between two companies (and two countries), Chalhoub can collect a "toll" on this knowledge: it can learn something from LVMH that it doesn't learn from Puig and then create something new with this knowledge.

Alliance Portfolio Summaries

When a firm's alliance portfolio is as large as Samsung's or Sony's, it's not easy to glean valuable insights from such simplified pictures. Since a big part of gaining second-degree network advantage comes from properly matching the portfolio configuration (hub-and-spoke, integrated or hybrid) with the specifics of the company and industry, making the distinction between these three portfolios involves looking at the proportion of alliance partners that are themselves interconnected. We've devised a very simple method for summarizing this information when there are a lot of partners involved. The full "spider web" pictures of Sony's and Samsung's portfolios shown in Chapter 2, for instance, are too complicated to use for this level of second-degree configuration analysis.

To make comparing the Sony and Samsung alliance portfolios easier, Figure 5.2 shows a series of bar graphs you can create based on their alliance portfolio pictures (see Figures 2.3 and 2.4 in Chapter 2). Recall from Chapter 4 that open ties are the relationships with partners that are not connected to other partners. Hub-and-spoke networks contain only open ties. Closed ties are the relationships with partners that are connected to other partners. Integrated networks contain only closed ties. A hybrid network will contain some open and some closed ties. The more open ties a hybrid network has, the more it leans toward a hub-and-spoke configuration; the more closed ties a hybrid network has, the more it leans toward the integrated configuration.

Figure 5.2: Second-degree summary for Samsung and Sony

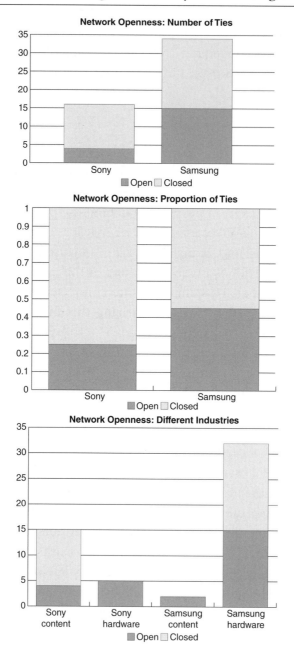

Counting and Comparing the Number of Open and Closed Ties

Using this knowledge and the portfolio pictures from Chapter 2 (Figures 2.3 and 2.4), count the number of open ties and closed ties for each company and then create the bar graphs. Figure 2.3 shows only 4 of Sony's 16 alliance partners are unconnected to the others; the rest are interconnected. So, that means Sony has 4 open ties and 12 closed ties. For Samsung, Figure 2.4 shows 15 open ties and 19 closed ties. By putting this information into a bar graph, we can easily see that Samsung's network is more hub-and-spoke than Sony's. Samsung has more partners in total, and more of these partners are connected to Samsung through open ties.

This point is made even more clearly by showing the proportion of ties, as in the second panel of Figure 5.2. Here, we see that Sony's portfolio is more integrated because it has a higher proportion of interconnected partners:

- Sony: 75% closed ties
- Samsung: 56% closed ties

This proportion-of-ties approach is useful when comparing two firms, or two divisions of a firm, based on the number of open ties, particularly when the total sizes of the portfolios differ due to size or nature of the businesses. For example, pharmaceutical firms make extensive use of alliances for innovation, but you cannot necessarily look at the sheer number of open ties as an indicator that a firm's alliance portfolio is hub-and-spoke. Pharmaceutical firms differ widely in size, and they also differ in the number of therapeutic areas that they cover. A larger firm or one with broader coverage would have more open ties in total as a sheer function of size and scope, so the proportion of open ties is a better indication of a hub-and-spoke configuration.

Classifying Ties by Industry or Alliance Purpose

In order to gain additional insights, let's make this analysis slightly more elaborate. You can also classify a firm's alliance partners into groups based on the industry they belong to. This is useful because alliances across different industries are often used to gain novel information, and a firm that lets these ties be open has more leverage relative to its partners than one that has closed ties to the same industry. This classification task may be hard when a partner is engaged in multiple industries, but you can draw useful conclusions by comparing alliances with similar purposes.

In Sony's case, there are two groups of partners—those helping the company to manufacture hardware (including Hitachi, Toshiba and Sharp) and those helping the company to deal with content (including Vivendi, Warner Music, and Baidu). All of the 5 hardware partners have closed ties, and 11 out of 15 content partners have closed ties. So, based on having a majority of closed ties, Sony's portfolio is more integrated. This information is summarized in the third panel of Figure 5.2.

Most of Samsung's partners manufacture hardware and nearly half of these partners (15 out of 32 partners) have open ties. This information is also summarized in the third panel of Figure 5.2. Samsung's only content alliance is a three-way alliance with Technicolor (owned by Thomson) and DreamWorks which has closed ties because the three firms work together. This three-way alliance is aimed at using Samsung's hardware expertise to make 3D home entertainment solutions such as a 3D-capable HDTV and a 3D Blu-ray disc player. It presents the DreamWorks' film *Monsters vs. Aliens* in a 3D Blu-ray version, which was produced by Technicolor. This alliance will also provide other films and trailers in 3D form.

Based on industry dynamism, one of the three factors in the Configuration Analysis Tool, here's what the bar graphs should look like:

- For a firm in a stable industry where highly reliable production is needed, the bar graph should be dominated by closed ties, which indicates an integrated portfolio configuration.
- For a firm in a dynamic industry where innovation is needed, the bar graph should show more open ties, which indicates a hub-and-spoke portfolio configuration.

In the case of Sony and Samsung, the hardware and content areas both demand innovation, yet Sony's portfolio is integrated for both of these industries. From these bar graphs analyzing Sony's portfolio you can see one reason why Sony is missing out on many opportunities to innovate. Since nearly half of Samsung's hardware ties are open and Sony has no open ties in hardware, Samsung has more innovation opportunities in hardware than Sony.

Another important issue to consider is whether a company can actually take resources and knowledge across partners in one industry and use them in relationships with partners in another industry, de facto acting as a broker of information and resources across different industries. Sony was in a good position to be a bridge between the content providers and the hardware manufacturers, and it should have been able to produce a product similar to the iPhone much earlier than Apple. However, this position didn't help because Sony apparently had high internal barriers that prevented the people working on hardware from sharing information with people working on content. Samsung has much lower access to content than Sony, but it is actually working on acting as a bridge between its content and hardware partners to use the knowledge it develops through collaborations on hardware (as well as that available internally) to benefit its collaborations with the content partners. Later on, in Chapter 10, we'll discuss how companies should coordinate their alliance activities internally in order to take advantage of these brokerage opportunities.

Figure 5.3: Steps in the Second-Degree Assessment Tool

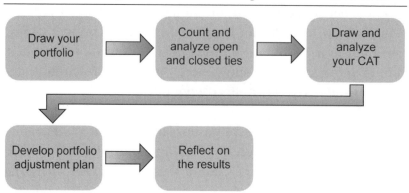

Visualizing Your Firm's Second Degree

Now you're well equipped to analyze your firm from the second-degree perspective. In this section, we'll take you through the specific, practical steps you need to visualize your firm's second-degree network advantage. Figure 5.3 shows the steps involved to complete the Second-Degree Assessment Tool exercise, which you can find in the Toolbox.

Step 1: Draw a Simplified or a Full Picture of Your Alliance Portfolio

This step will help you get a visual image of your portfolio. If you have fewer than 12 partners, then you can draw a full picture of your alliance portfolio. In this picture you depict each partner with a circle and draw the connections between them. You may end up with a "spider web" picture and that's fine. To make the picture more informative, indicate the key insights you gained from the First-Degree-Assessment exercise: each partner's rating for the Four Dimensions of Fit and the key benefits your company gets from each partner.

If your alliance portfolio has more than 12 partners, you can depict your alliance portfolio in a simplified form. You can use Figure 5.1 as an example. Group similar small partners together in the same way we depicted "Retailers in the Middle East" in one circle of the Chalhoub Group's portfolio picture. Use lines to draw connections between the groups of partners.

Step 2: Count and Analyze Open and Closed Ties

When you complete this step, you'll determine the alliance portfolio configuration your firm has now. If you opted for drawing a full picture of your alliance portfolio, count the number of open and closed ties just as we did for Sony and Samsung earlier in this chapter. Create the bar graphs as shown in Figure 5.2.

If you drew a simplified version of your alliance portfolio, then you still need to think whether your partners are connected. If all of your partners in a particular circle are unconnected, then you can count them as open ties; if they tend to work with each other, then they are closed ties.

If your firm operates in more than one industry, use the questions in the box to analyze your ties by industry group.

Questions to Analyze Your Industry Ties

- What are the principal industries in which your firm competes?
- Which partners help your firm succeed in each industry?
- What does your firm's portfolio configuration look like for each industry? Are the ties mostly open or closed?

Step 3: Use the Configuration Alignment Tool (CAT)

Now use the CAT to determine the configuration your alliance portfolio should have. Examine the dynamism and nature of uncertainty facing your industry, evaluate the breadth of your firm's product or service range, and assess its market power. Use the following questions as a guide.

Questions to Build Your Configuration Alignment Tool (CAT)

- What is the level of dynamism facing your industry?
  - How much volatility exists with respect to supply and demand?
  - How hard is it to predict the direction of industry change or the likelihood of disruptive innovations?
- What is the range of your firm's product or service offering?
  - How specialized or broad is your range of products and services?
  - How well does your firm handle diversity of ideas, processes, and resources?
- How much market power does your firm wield in the industry?
  - Does your firm have high or low market share?
  - As compared to other firms in your industry, does your firm have minimal or major financial resources?

Now mark your firm's answers on the CAT. If most of your answers are to the left-hand side of this grid, then your portfolio needs to be integrated, in other words you benefit if your partners work together. If most of your answers are at the center, then you need a hybrid portfolio. That is, you will benefit when some of your partners are connected, while others are not. If most answers are at the right-hand side of this grid, then your portfolio needs to be mostly hub-and-spoke. That is, you benefit from being the broker among disconnected partners.

Step 4: Develop Portfolio Adjustment Plan

The next step is to draw your current alliance portfolio and compare it to the "ideal" configuration network determined by the CAT analysis in step 3. This comparison is the key to thinking strategically about your alliance network and achieving network-based competitive advantage: you need to think about how to make your network more integrated or more hub-and-spoke. This exercise is also of value, because it aggregates all of the information about your alliances into a single visual picture that will enable people in your organization to understand who your firm's partners are, what the rationale is for each individual relationship, and whether your overall alliance portfolio supports your firm's strategy. In addition, if you know what you are getting from each partner, you can also think about the brokerage opportunities that could exist if you used the knowledge and resources from one partner in dealing with the other partners.

Key Questions for Developing a Portfolio Adjustment Plan

- Does your current alliance portfolio match your ideal network?
- What new alliance formations or terminations will improve your alliance portfolio (closer to the CAT ideal)?
- Would encouraging alliances among some of your partners improve your alliance portfolio?

Step 5: Reflect on the Results

In this step you reflect about the key learnings from the exercise.

In the following sections, we'll describe how to build more open or closed ties and provide questions you can use to identify opportunities to form the types of ties you need.

Key Questions for Reflection

- What gaps in your knowledge of your firm's alliance portfolio did this exercise reveal?
- Where can you get information to fill in these gaps in your knowledge?
- Is your firm's alliance portfolio optimal for your industry and your firm's strategy?
- How frequently will your network position change due to alliance formations and terminations in your industry?

Five ways to Build Open Ties

Let's say you discover that your firm's alliance portfolio is too integrated and you need to increase the number of open ties. You can do this by thinking through the following five partnering recommendations, which are summarized in Figure 5.4.

1. Partner with Complementors

Complementors make a product or service that enhances the value of your products or services. Software is a complement for hardware, a 3D movie Blu-ray disc player is a complement for a home cinema system. Firms tend to overlook makers of complements because they often operate in different industries. There's

Figure 5.4: Five ways to build open ties

---

1. Partner with complementors

2. Partner with substitutes

3. Partner with new industry entrants

4. Partner with your partners' competitors

5. Partner with your direct competitors

a reason why Samsung cooperates with DreamWorks and Technicolor: it wants to learn how to make 3D content so it can create and sell more 3D-capable hardware. Similarly, Intel processors may power the 3D hardware, but Intel lacks knowledge about making 3D movies. So Samsung acts as a bridge between Intel and DreamWorks. Kia Motors makes cars which provide a complement for Samsung's products, such as the Galaxy Tab. In fact, the alliance with Kia helps Samsung learn how to design its Galaxy Tab to act as a control and navigation device for Kia cars.

We worked with a Thai company that made light alcoholic beverages for women. After one of its executives suggested the idea of marketing the beverages at spas, the company decided to form alliances with a taxi firm and a spa chain. The company planned to provide phone numbers of preferred taxi services on the packaging of its bottles so the consumers would be sure they were driven home by reputable taxi drivers. Since spa chains did not usually use preferred taxi companies, this allowed the Thai beverage company to build a hub-and-spoke network with open ties to these two partners.

To identify opportunities to partner with makers of complements, use the following questions.

Questions to Find Makers of Complements

- What products or services make your own product or service more valuable?
- Which firms make these products/services?
- Which of these firms don't work with your current partners?
- Of the firms which don't work with your current partners, which ones have the highest strategy, resource, organization, and culture fit with your firm?
- How could you transfer the knowledge you obtain in dealing with these new partners to your other partners who don't work with them?

2. Partner with Makers of Substitutes

Substitutes are the products and services which make your products and services much less valuable. These are not products of direct competitors who make the same product or service as you. The Wii gaming console developed by Nintendo is a substitute product for fitness centers. This device enables people to move around as they play video games, such as boxing or tennis. Conversely, a substitute product for the Wii is actually going to the gym. If Nintendo aligned with a gym chain to promote using the Wii during regular workouts, this would be an example of partnering with a firm that offers substitute services. And the probability would be very high that no other video game maker aligns itself with a gym chain.

Use the following questions to identify makers of substitutes you could approach to form alliances with.

Questions to Find Makers of Substitutes

- What products or services do your customers use instead of your own product or service?
- What makes customers switch from your product or service to these substitutes?
- Which firms make these substitute products or services?
- Of these firms, which ones have the highest strategy, resource, organization, and culture fit with your firm?
- What new business model could you build if you were to connect your business with the business of a substitute maker?
- How could you transfer the knowledge you obtain in dealing with these new partners to your other partners who don't work with them?

3. Partner with New Industry Entrants

Firms that are new to the industry often have a hard time finding partners. However, these firms could have just the right innovations established firms are looking for. Consider this example from the computer graphics animation industry. Pixar was the pioneer in this industry, but it was also the new kid on the block with no major partners. By partnering with Pixar, Disney got access to Pixar's technology and talent, and this allowed Disney to learn about computer graphics animation.

To think about opportunities for forming alliances with new firms, ask the following questions.

Questions for Identifying New Industry Entrants

- What firms have been the new entrants in your industry over the past three years?
- What capabilities does each of these new entrants have?
- What information or resources can these firms provide to you?
- Which of these firms have the highest strategy, resource, organization, and culture fit with your firm?
- Are your existing partners already working with these entrants?
- If not, how can you form relationships with the ones that are not connected to your existing partners?
- How could you transfer the knowledge you obtain in dealing with these new partners to your other partners who don't work with them?

---

4. Partner with Your Partners' Competitors

Beginning in the 1990s there was a lot of talk in the computer industry about Wintel—the collaborative relationship between

Microsoft and Intel. As makers of complementary products, they worked closely with each other to establish the dominant position in the PC market. Even though these companies had to collaborate to increase the value of their technological platforms and elbow out competing technologies (including Apple's), they also competed for how much of this value each one got to keep. Despite the fact that Microsoft depended on Intel's success, it also worked with Intel's arch-rival: AMD. Microsoft frequently demanded, for example, that Intel share with AMD its new chip-making technologies, which Intel had spent millions of dollars developing. Since Intel did not collaborate with AMD, Microsoft used its open ties to both firms to play them off against each other. This situation continued for years and may still be going on as you read this. For example, in 2011, Microsoft talked about partnering with other chip makers, such as Nvidia, to incorporate their products into Microsoft's tablet PCs.[1] If Intel doesn't have an alliance with Nvidia, then Microsoft's tie with this firm would be an open tie.[2]

To form an open tie this way, you need to know who your partners' rivals are. What will you gain by forming ties with some of them? It's clear that to pull off this strategy, you need to have more market power than your partners. To harmonize this potentially unstable relationship and reduce hostilities between your partners, you can ask them to focus their activities on different segments of the same line of business. Hewlett Packard had two alliance partners that were rivals in the making of printer cartridges. HP kept the balance between them by asking one partner to focus its R&D on making high-end cartridges while another partner was asked to focus on driving the costs of basic cartridges

[1] http://news.cnet.com/8301-10805_3-57520885-75/trouble-in
-paradise-cracks-show-in-microsoft-intel-alliance/.
[2] http://www.anandtech.com/show/4409/windows-8-on-amd-intel
-nvidia-qualcomm-ti-let-the-race-begin.

down. Even though these partners were rivals, HP could guarantee each one of them enough business so that they were reasonably happy but also not 100% comfortable due to the presence of their rival in HP's alliance portfolio.

To think about opportunities for forming alliances with your partners' competitors, ask the following questions.

Questions to Partner with Your Partners' Competitors

- Who are the competitors of your current partners?
- Which competitors are likely to be more cooperative than the others?
- What benefits in terms of exchanging information and resources can you obtain from collaborating with these competitors?
- Can you get a power advantage over your current partners by joining forces with these competitors?
- What degree of strategy, resource, organization, and culture fit does this firm have with your firm?
- How could you transfer the knowledge you obtain in dealing with these new partners to your other partners who don't work with them?

---

5. Partner with Your Direct Competitors

In their attempt to differentiate from one another, competitors often form relationships with partners who don't work together. This creates a situation where competitors have non-overlapping alliance networks. However, if you are looking for an open tie, a partnership with your competitor is likely to provide you with just that. Remember how Lufthansa operated in two airline alliances at the same time—Oneworld and Star Alliance? Lufthansa accomplished this by buying the BMI airline (see Chapter 4).

Partnerships with direct competitors can be risky because they may create opportunities for information or resource leakage. However, these ties can definitely provide you with ideas on how things are done differently in a company that competes for the same clients. These partnerships can also allow you an opportunity to join forces in fighting other common competitors. In so doing, you would be inspired by the Godfather Don Corleone's advice: "keep your friends close but your enemies closer." Between the 1980s and 2000s, Enel, an Italian energy firm, and EDF, the French energy firm, formed a series of alliances, first to sell French energy in Italy and then to do joint research on nuclear energy. Enel now has a representative office in France and EDF has a representative office in Italy. This collaboration has greater objectives than just mutual learning—the two companies also work together to withstand competition from other competitors, namely the German utility firms.[3]

Questions to Partner with Your Direct Competitors

- Which competitor of yours is likely to be more cooperative than the others?
- What degree of fit (e.g. strategy, resource, organization, and culture) does this firm have with your firm?
- What benefits in terms of exchanging information and resources can you obtain from collaborating with this competitor?
- Can you get a power advantage by joining forces with this competitor in order to fight some other firms?
- How could you transfer the knowledge you obtain in dealing with this new partner to your other partners who don't work with it?

---

[3] Soda, G., M. Bergami, and P. Celli. 2012. *National Monopoly to Successful Multinational: The Case of Enel.* Palgrave Macmillan.

Figure 5.5: Four ways to build closed ties

---

1. **Make referrals**

2. **Neutralize a broker**

3. **Seek referrals**

4. **Form a union**

Four Ways to Build Closed Ties

You may discover that your firm's alliance portfolio is not integrated enough and you need to increase the number of closed ties. To do this, consider these four recommendations which are summarized in Figure 5.5.

As a general rule, you build a closed tie when you collaborate with two partners at the same time or when you trade referrals with your partners. In academic research on alliances, groups of three firms are often called "triads." Sounds a bit like a branch of a Chinese criminal organization, huh? But this is not what the "triad" label is meant to convey. Simply put, a triad is a group of three firms, and a closed triad has three firms that are connected to each other.

1. Make Referrals

This is the simplest way to form closed ties. Basically, it involves working with two partners who don't currently work with each other. If you want to have more closed ties in your alliance portfolio, suggest that these partners work with each other on some project and this part of your alliance portfolio becomes integrated. Toyota does this with its suppliers in Japan. When it forms a tie with a new supplier, it asks this supplier to exchange equity stakes with its other suppliers so that this supplier's success becomes dependent upon the other suppliers' success. Suppliers are encouraged to learn from each other and transfer the best practices, and this development of trust between suppliers contributes to the development of trust in Toyota's entire alliance portfolio.

To follow this strategy, you need to determine which of your existing partners can benefit the most by working together. It's useful to begin by thinking about your partners that have strategy, resource, organization, and culture fit with each other. Then sit down with them and think of projects that they could work on which will further your business interests. The more partners you introduce to each other, the more your alliance portfolio will be integrated.

2. Neutralize a Broker

What if you are in a situation where you have a partner that is playing you off against another partner to which you are not connected? In other words, what if your firm is like AMD with an open tie to Microsoft, which has an open tie to Intel, but there is no tie between AMD and Intel? In this scenario, Microsoft can be considered a broker between Intel and AMD because it is playing off Intel against AMD. To neutralize Microsoft's brokerage advantage, Intel and AMD could agree to form a direct alliance between themselves. Now, this may sound like a difficult strategy to implement, and due to the bad blood between Intel and AMD, it may be a true impossibility. However, if the two competitors can agree that it is better to collaborate than to be continuously played off against one another by the broker, then they can capture a lot of value for themselves.

Here's another example. The Toronto Maple Leafs (TML), a Canadian hockey club worth about a billion dollars, generates much of its revenues from broadcasts of its games on the cable networks. Two Canadian cable providers broadcast the majority of the TML games: Bell and Rogers Communications. TML has been playing these competitors off one another for a long time by extracting greater payments (and other better terms) for broadcasting its games. When the two cable companies got tired of fighting over TML, they agreed to create a joint venture that would buy 70% of TML and then jointly determine the terms and scheduling of the broadcasts. Now, TML has to play by the rules dictated to it by Rogers and Bell.

If you find yourself in a situation like Bell or Rogers, you will benefit from this strategy. Do you have an important customer or a supplier that is always playing you off against a rival of yours by trying to extract better terms for their contracts? If this customer (or supplier) is truly negatively impacting your bottom line, then perhaps you need to talk to your rival, who also might not be very happy about this partner's behavior. You may gain something by overcoming your past rivalries and joining an alliance with your rival to neutralize the advantage of this "broker."

3. Seek Referrals

A variation on the "make a referral" strategy involves forming a tie with a new partner by using a referral from your existing partner. In other words, if you want to form a tie to a new firm, find out whether one of your existing partners knows someone who works in the new firm. Then, explore whether the new firm could achieve synergies by working in collaboration with you and your existing partner to serve a partner of its own.

By knowing the research on how referrals facilitate new alliance formations, INSEAD used this strategy to build a new education program in Russia that it would likely not have established on its own. In 2011, INSEAD started delivering this unique year-long executive education program designed to train a 500-person class of top executives every year for several years using both the usual face-to-face teaching methods and

web-based tools. After only five years this program will generate 2,500 alumni, and all of these executives will come from
the same company! The client company is Sberbank, the largest
player in the Russian retail, commercial, and investment banking
sector.[4] To make this program and partnership happen, INSEAD
approached Sberbank not on its own, but rather in cooperation
with the New Economic School (NES) in Russia which had good
contacts in Sberbank. Since NES knew INSEAD and Sberbank
knew NES, the NES referral connected INSEAD to Sberbank. In
this way, INSEAD formed a "triad" with Sberbank and NES
which involves a high degree of trust and mutual knowledge
sharing. As a result of this cooperation, this triad created an
extremely successful new program.

4. Form a Union

In 1981, three French insurance companies—MAIF, MAAF, and
MACIF—created a multi-party joint venture called Intermutuelles
Assistance (IA) to achieve economies of scale in processing
customers' claims. If you are insured by one of these companies
and your car breaks down, you call IA not your insurer. IA's
customer care representatives dispatch the assistance truck and
help process your claims. Or, if you injure your leg due to a
ski accident in the Alps, IA sends the medical team to help you
and IA finds a driver to bring you home to the exotic French
village of Bourron Marlotte, for example. The three partners
outsource all non-core activities to the joint venture and accu-
mulate significant savings as a result. By 2011, there were 12
members participating in this joint venture, as many other
insurance companies discovered the benefits of pooling their
resources in this initiative.

---

[4] http://www.sbrf.ru/en/about/socialresponsibility/employees/
leaders/.

This strategy involves moving away from triads toward forming multi-party alliances. To profit from this strategy, you need to have a group of competitors who perform the same tasks and who can gain economies of scale by centralizing their operations. However, these common activities don't have to be in the area of improving operational efficiencies only. Firms in knowledge-intensive industries often form "patenting unions;" that is, they jointly patent multiple inventions in a particular domain to deter new firms from doing research there. This way the economy of scale originates from pooling the results of joint research.

Going Forward

Now you have the background, tools, and tips to analyze and build your second-degree network advantage. In the next two chapters, we will examine how to use the third-degree perspective to access third-degree network advantage benefits. Specifically, we will explore the concept of your firm's status and present the tools you can use to gauge your firm's status position in its industry and enhance it.

Chapter Highlights

- Visualizing your firm's portfolio from the second-degree perspective can help you see whether your firm has an optimal alliance portfolio configuration.
- Counting and analyzing the open ties can help you understand to what degree there will be opportunities for breakthrough innovation in your current alliance portfolio.
- Counting and analyzing the closed ties can help you understand to what degree your firm will have opportunities for mutual learning and support from a group of partners.

- If your alliance portfolio configuration is different from the ideal one indicated by using the Configuration Alignment Tool, you need to change it by adding open or closed ties.
- To build more open-tie relationships, your firm can form alliances with these five types of new partners:
  - makers of complements
  - makers of substitutes
  - new industry entrants
  - your partners' competitors
  - your direct competitors
- To build more closed-tie relationships, your firm can take these four actions:
  - make referrals
  - neutralize a broker
  - seek referrals
  - form a union

CHAPTER SIX

THE THIRD-DEGREE PERSPECTIVE: ACHIEVING THE STATUS ADVANTAGE

Many people around the world remember November 22, 1963 as the date of U.S. President John F. Kennedy's assassination in Dallas, Texas. As dictated and legitimized by the Constitution and U.S. federal law, Vice President, Lyndon Johnson, assumed the Presidency immediately following confirmation of Kennedy's death. Even though Johnson had the title, he didn't immediately have command of a nation that idolized Kennedy and was plunged into frantic hysteria during this time of crisis and uncertainty. In other words, Johnson became the legitimate President in the eyes of the law well before he gained the respect of the people. He acted quickly to confirm his status as the new President using a method that was both brilliant and cruel.

In the ensuing chaos of the day and fearing more attacks, the Secret Service wanted to move President Johnson from the room at Parkland Memorial Hospital, where Kennedy's body lay, to Air Force One, which was considered a flying fortress. However, President Johnson refused to go until Mrs Kennedy was ready to leave, which meant waiting for President Kennedy's body to be fully examined and transported. Once they moved to Air Force One, Johnson again refused to leave until both Mrs

Kennedy and her husband's body were on board. Airplane seats had to be taken out to make room for the coffin, further delaying departure and compromising the security offered when Air Force One is airborne. Why did President Johnson choose to remain exposed and vulnerable to other possible attempts to decapitate the U.S. government? By putting the well-being of the Kennedy family ahead of the country's security, was President Johnson simply thinking irrationally?

Photographs of President Johnson's swearing-in aboard Air Force One provide the answer. As the President raised his right hand to recite the oath of office, witnesses crowded around. The photographs show Johnson's wife, barely visible standing on his right, and Jackie Kennedy, still wearing the coat stained with her husband's blood, framed perfectly and standing prominently on his left. This ceremony occurred less than two hours after her husband was pronounced dead and not more than 20 feet from her husband's coffin.

From a legal standpoint, Mrs Kennedy didn't need to be present at the swearing-in. In fact, it was also unnecessary to conduct the ceremony before returning to the White House. However, President Johnson seized the opportunity to use Mrs Kennedy's status to legitimize his Presidency.[1] At this time, many considered the Kennedy family to be the closest thing to royalty in the United States, and Americans admired Mrs Kennedy as much as her husband. Standing next to President Johnson served as more than just a symbolic gesture of Mrs Kennedy's support: her presence confirmed Johnson's status.

Like President Johnson, businesses can gain status through their alliance networks because the influence of high-status firms extends to their partners. To see your firm's alliance network—the network of ties connecting all firms in your

---

[1] Caro, R.A. 2012. Annals of History, "The Transition." *The New Yorker*, April 2, p. 32.

industry and beyond—you want to fully broaden your field of vision (adjust the microscope lens again) to incorporate the third-degree perspective.

In this chapter, we define alliance network status and describe the advantages associated with this property of the third-degree perspective. We explain the conditions under which network status is most valuable to organizations, and we discuss when firms should have high- or low-status partners in their alliance portfolios. Both can be valuable assets to an organization when blended in the right proportions. Because other firms want to connect to those firms that have high status, one key advantage of high status is the freedom to shape the alliance network around your firm. Status also has more direct advantages because customers value products and services more highly when they come from a high-status company.

What is a Firm's Status?

We can all name firms that hold prestigious positions in their industries. They are leaders among others, are able to influence industry trends and attention, and are used as benchmarks for comparison. If you are asked to quickly list a few of these firms, which come to mind? When we ask participants in executive training programs in North America, they mention firms like Coca-Cola, Apple, and Starbucks. Our European participants gravitate to BMW, Nestlé, and Unilever among others. And in Asia we hear names such as Samsung, Canon, and Singapore Airlines. What's common across all of these companies is that they are not only financially successful relative to others in their industries but they are also known for producing quality products and services over a long history. They are perceived to have unique and valuable capabilities underlying this reputation for quality and have used their positions to influence the directions of their industries.

You don't need to know the network position of a firm to be able to tell its status, although you will immediately recognize Samsung, mentioned above, as a high-status firm that also has a strong hub-and-spoke network. Status also matters because it influences how firms and individuals in networks interact with each other. Consider the towns in Roman Britannia again. By looking at the road network shown in Figure I.1, we can see why Londinium would receive more visitors even if people moved randomly from town to town. It's at the center of a hub-and-spoke highway network and people need to pass through Londinium to go elsewhere. But people do not move randomly from town to town. They travel when they have a purpose for doing so, and they need to make sure they are going to the place most likely to fulfill that purpose.

Based on what you already know about Londinium, where would you go if you were in Roman Britannia and needed to make a trade of rare goods? Even if you were located midway between Venta Belgarum (Winchester) and Londinium and could go to either town, you would know that Londinium was the more important town, and you would assume (rightly) that it was also a better place for trading goods. You would also have predicted (correctly) that the right people to complete your trade (in other words buyers or experts in your product) would also be attracted to Londinium. Similarly, even within an alliance network the high-status firm becomes the "go-to" place because others assume it is more capable.

Characteristics That Contribute to Status

A firm's status is based in part on comparison of its characteristics with those of other firms. Many characteristics can contribute positively to status, but these four are especially important and usually related to each other:

- financial success
- possession of valuable capabilities
- quality products/services
- reputation for honest dealings.

Those firms identified as having high status enjoy advantages unavailable to others. In particular, they are attractive alliance partners—other firms want to gain access to their high-quality products/services or underlying capabilities. High-status firms also have the advantage of credibility—when they voice their ideas others are more willing to listen and follow. In general, high status provides all the benefits associated with having influence and being a leader.

Firms with higher quality products or services are most likely to achieve high status in the long run. However, it's possible to see a gap between status and quality products or services in the short and medium terms. Over long periods of time it is difficult to maintain a large gap, but there can be gaps because judging quality is a task made difficult by inaccurate or incomplete information. For this reason, status is not a direct result of a firm's characteristics.

A quality–status gap can persist because the human brain is hardwired to make judgments and evaluations regardless of information access. We want to put everything in a category—good or bad, big or small, high or low status. Even if we lack enough direct evidence to make an accurate assessment, we grasp for any available cues or proxies upon which we can assess others. For example, think about how we evaluate learning in our children's schools. Without being in the classroom to observe the actual learning process we use other signs to judge learning quality including student–teacher ratio, number of books in the classroom, teachers' credentials, and so on. These factors do not guarantee learning, but we think they are correlated with learning.

Figure 6.1: How status is generated

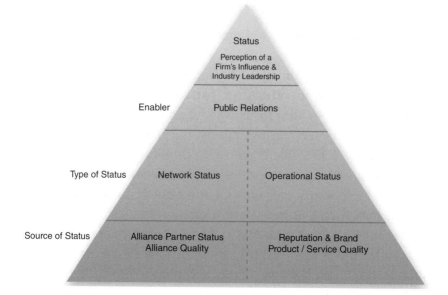

Operational and Network Status

Figure 6.1 shows how overall firm status is generated and indicates that status has two main components or types: operational status and network status.

- **Operational status** is related to the actual quality of a firm's products and/or services. It results from how well the firm has delivered in the past and is reflected in its corporate reputation and brand.
- **Network status** is a product of the quality of a firm's alliances, which in turn is judged by whether it has high-status firms as alliance partners. Network status is also influenced by what happens in the firm's alliances, if that is known. Do the firm's alliances last, are they successful, and does the firm behave well as a partner?

As Figure 6.1 further illustrates, firms can use public relations to make sure that others (such as buyers, suppliers, and partners) have the best possible perceptions of the firm's operational and network status. We discuss the role of public relations in greater detail in Chapter 7.

An organization's overall corporate reputation is an expectation that it will do something which it has done before; in other words, supply outstanding service, provide transparent and full disclosure, develop leading-edge products, and so on. Reputation is a prediction about an organization's behavior based on the past. For example, a bank that has withstood the recent global financial crisis may gain a reputation among its community, investors, government, and customers for being a good investment and trusted driver of economic growth.

A firm's brand is closely related to reputation but is specific to how customers perceive an organization's products/services. Perrier, a brand of water sold by the Nestlé Company, is perceived to have a "distinctly fresh and clean taste." Similarly, customers view Wal-Mart as offering "low prices on leading products." Apple is known for innovations, and Nike's motto, "Just do it," reflects its perceived association with winning. A brand confers an organization's identity and conveys its product/service qualities to customers.

In the world of alliances, network status projects the organization's overall quality reputation to a wide range of outsiders who attempt to evaluate it. It influences whether potential alliance partners judge the organization to be cooperative, whether banks appraise it as a good loan risk, and whether environmental stakeholders judge the organization's pollution abatement strategy as credible.

Status versus Brand

Status is similar to reputation and brand, which are better known and understood terms, but it differs in two important ways.

First, an important component of status is derived from the firm's alliances—its network status. That is, your network status is determined by the company you choose to keep and not to keep. A popular cue used to judge you or your organization's quality is the quality of those willing to associate with you. The decision-making shortcut is to assume that if high-quality people or organizations are your partners, then you must be of high quality too. So, having many ties to high-status partners will increase your status—you will be perceived to be of higher quality as well. The opposite is also true. Building an association with a low-status partner will reduce your own status. In some situations the consequences of low-status associations can be devastating. J. Willard Marriott understood the power of status when he coined the phrase, "Choose your friends wisely—they will make or break you."

Monitor Group chose its friends unwisely. This prestigious global consulting firm counted a vast array of corporate giants as clients. However, on November 7, 2012 it declared bankruptcy. From its beginning in 1983, Monitor had a high-status ranking among clients and potential MBA recruits. The founding partners were connected to Harvard, and this status-building association created an image of academic competence and analytical rigor even though there was no formal alliance with Harvard. Mere association can create network status and Monitor Group benefited from that. In 2008, when the consulting industry was hit hard by the global financial crisis and had to take steps to weather the storm, Monitor Group directed more resources toward government consulting to replace lost corporate revenues. It accepted a consulting project to help Muammar Gaddafi's Libyan government improve its image, but according to *The Economist's* report on Monitor Group's demise, "the engagement ended up damaging its own [image]."[2] Existing and

---

[2] *The Economist.* 2012. Monitor's end. November 14.

potential clients questioned Monitor Group's own judgment and ability to deliver high-quality advice.

Second, status is a ranking—a pecking order—which determines relative merit. Status involves comparisons, where some will be seen as better than others. We see this idea played out in high-school cliques or in caste systems, which establish hierarchies of social classes to separate groups, set relative roles and provide opportunities for some groups, and impose restrictions on others. In India, there are several major castes: Brahmin, Kshatriya, Vaishya, Shudra, and Untouchable. This ideological scheme was theoretically composed of 3,000 sub-castes, which in turn claimed to be composed of 90,000 local sub-groups.[3] Companies do the same. For example, investment banks take status into account when they make syndicates and allocate roles to each syndicate member. High-status law firms are more flexible in market entry than law firms in the tier below them.[4]

Researchers have illustrated the power of status in many different settings. A central insight is that if two people or organizations perform a task to the same quality level, the one with higher status will receive greater recognition. Status enhances, and sometimes even exaggerates, perceptions of one's performance and potential. Robert Merton studied the effects of status on the amount of recognition scientists receive for their research. Publishing articles in science journals involves extensive review processes that screen out all but the most insightful and credible studies. Despite this pre-screening,

---

[3] http://en.wikipedia.org/wiki/Caste_system_in_India#Modern_status _of_the_caste_system.

[4] For law firms, see Phillips, D. J. and E.W. Zuckerman. 2002. Middle-status conformity: Theoretical restatement and empirical demonstration in two markets. *American Journal of Sociology* 107: 379–429. The investment studies were by Joel Podolny, and are discussed in more detail below.

Merton found that the journal articles written by high-status scientists were read more widely than those of lower status scientists. In fact, when articles were co-authored by both a high- and low-status scientist, the high-status scientist was automatically given more credit for the collaborative effort. Merton's findings show that status leads to attributions about relative ability, effort, and performance.[5]

Status rankings are an extremely powerful force in networks of all kinds including, of course, alliance networks. Some researchers argue that a low-status ranking will lead to low-level performance. That is, status rankings create a self-fulfilling prophecy so that we adjust our effort and performance to fit with our status levels. In the late 1930s, William F. Whyte spent more than three years living among Italian immigrants in the slums of Boston and observed the social dynamics of gang members.[6] He noticed that the gang members' bowling scores were aligned with their relative status rankings. The high-status gang members were consistently better bowlers. Unless bowling skills enhance one's abilities to excel at other gang-related activities, it seems that the pecking order influenced bowling scores and the lower status gang members were more willing to lose games to the higher status ones.

Status Association: The Company a Firm Keeps

Status associations are used in the same way to evaluate organizations. Joel Baum and Christine Oliver studied daycare facilities in Toronto. They found that the parents' perceptions of daycare facilities in the area were colored by their relationships with other organizations: A facility associated with an

---

[5] Merton, R.K. 1968. The Matthew effect in science. *Science* 159: 56–63.

[6] Whyte, W.F. 1943. *Street Corner Society*. University of Chicago Press.

established school or church was viewed to be providing better childcare as compared to a facility that lacked such associations.[7]

We should expect this result because we form opinions about the status of a firm by the company it keeps, just as we judge individuals by their company. We expect a high-status firm to be connected, for example by strategic alliances or buyer–supplier relationships, to another high-status firm, rather than a low-status one. Thus, for managers considering the ideal alliance portfolio, high status gives opportunities. The high-status firms can get relationships with other firms freely and easily because they are desired partners.

Because we judge firms by the company they keep, firms need to choose partners carefully. Too many relationships with low-status firms can hurt high-status firms, just as connections with high-status firms can help firms of low status. For example, investment banks carefully guard their status by managing their relationships with other banks. When a company like Facebook wants to raise capital, it will hire investment banks to underwrite the sale of its stock. Investment banks often work together in syndicates to share risk and reach a larger number of investors. When choosing partners they try to maximize the number of high-status banks in the syndicate, and it is not uncommon for these banks to turn down invitations to participate with lower status banks in underwriting syndicates.

It used to be common to announce syndicates through advertisements known as "tombstones." The "tombstone" was a list of banks contributing capital to the new issue. The list of banks on the "tombstone" was organized in a particular order, with the banks playing a more prominent role in the issue listed

---

[7] Baum, J.A.C. and C. Oliver. 1992. Institutional embeddedness and the dynamics of organizational populations. *American Sociological Review* 57(4): 540–559.

first followed by the banks that had a less prominent role to play. The tombstones created an additional problem: high-status banks turned down invitations if their positions on the tombstone did not appropriately reflect the status order of the syndicate members. If a high-status bank participating in a public offering saw that its name listed below the names of other high-status banks or, worse, below the names of banks that it considered to be of lower status, the bank would lobby for rearranging the names on the tombstone or withdraw its capital from the new issue.

Why did high-status banks guard their positions on the tombstones so jealously? The organizational sociologist Joel Podolny found that banks knew that these positions signaled their leadership and influence in the industry. And, since suppliers of capital to the financial markets looked at these signals, they were more willing to lend the high-status banks money at lower interest rates. In other words, the higher status banks had lower costs of acquiring resources.[8] High-status investment banks also tend to have a higher share of the market for underwriting Initial Public Offerings because companies listing their securities prefer to be served by high-status bankers and investors looking for new securities also prefer to buy them from high-status banks.[9]

An organization's high status confers upon it a leadership position in the industry and in the alliance network. But, alliances with lower status players can harm an organization's

---

[8] Podolny, J.M. 1993. A status-based model of market competition. *American Journal of Sociology* 98: 829–872; Podolny, J.M. 1994. Market uncertainty and the social character of economic exchange. *Administrative Science Quarterly* 39(3): 458–470.

[9] Shipilov, A.V. 2005. Should you bank on your network? Relational and positional embeddedness in the making of financial capital. *Strategic Organization* 3(3): 279–309.

status. Consider the association between Apple as a designer of devices and Foxconn (also known as Hon Hai), the Taiwanese assembler. It is normal for brand-name firms such as Apple to build devices using lesser-known assemblers. Sometimes these assemblers are simply unknown outside the industry, but at other times they do become known and seen in a negative light. This is exactly what happened when the world learned about the Apple–Foxconn relationship at the same time that poor working conditions at Foxconn's factories became known. The employees were working long hours and were pressured to do a lot of overtime, lived in poor quality dormitories, and some were underage students from the local schools who were supposed to be studying instead of working.[10] These labor problems were enough to hurt Foxconn's status as an alliance partner and in turn to hurt Apple's status.

A product "designed in California" loses its allure if customers associate it with ill-treated workers in a Taiwanese-owned, mainland-China sweatshop.[11] Indeed, some customers set up advocacy groups to protest against the poor working conditions of Apple's suppliers.[12] This is why Apple sent its top officials to Foxconn to conduct inspections and to gain agreement on improvement of the working conditions. Apple needed to improve the Foxconn situation in order to prevent damage to its own status. It was not able to break off the relationship with Foxconn, at least in the short term, because Apple was too dependent on its assembly prowess.

---

[10] http://www.forbes.com/sites/susanadams/2012/09/12/apples-new-foxconn-embarrassment/.

[11] Vascellaro, J.A. 2012. Audit faults Apple supplier. *Wall Street Journal*, March 30.

[12] http://sumofus.org/campaigns/apple-uprising/.

Advantages of Network Status

Before we move on to discussing the specific, tangible advantages of status, let's recap four key points about status:

1. Status is a cue or proxy used to judge an organization's quality and abilities.
2. Status involves a rank ordering which means that an organization's status is perceived to be better or worse than others.
3. We judge an organization's ability to perform a given task by its status ranking; in other words by the company it keeps.
4. Because status ripples through relationships, an organization's status is determined by the status rankings of its alliance partners.

Monitor Group's status was greatly diminished by its engagement with the Libyan government and Muammar Gaddafi. Apple risks its status when it deals with controversial companies like Foxconn.

So far we have discussed status advantages in general terms—high status leads to perceptions that you perform at a high level and lead your industry. For organizations, this perception translates into three tangible advantages. These represent the third-degree network advantages—the information, cooperation, and power gained from being positively evaluated by others as a result of having a central position in the alliance network.

- **Information advantage:** Partners are likely to share more information with the high-status firm. This means that the high-status firm is well informed about what's going on in the industry. The high-status firm also doesn't need to spend as much money spreading information about its own activities. Because high status attracts attention, this makes the high-status firms the trendsetters in their industries and reduces their advertising costs.[13] Ideas of high-status firms also become more readily acceptable and their understanding of what is a "good quality product" becomes the industry norm.

- **Cooperation advantage:** High-status organizations are attractive alliance partners. Other organizations seek them out for partnerships because they not only view them as high-quality partners but would also enjoy a status-ranking increase for themselves. High-status organizations, therefore, have greater opportunities to enter alliances and to get more information from their current partners.[14] Their partners are also likely to invest a lot of effort to ensure that the relationship works. For example, in the Formula 1 racing competition, car makers were more likely to make performance-enhancing modifications to the engines of cars used by the high-status racing teams as compared to the engines of cars used by the low-status racing teams.[15]

- **Power advantage:** When high-status organizations make claims or requests, others are more likely to listen and acquiesce. This gives them greater influence in their industries. Because a high-quality employee would much rather work in a high-status firm than in a low-status firm, the employee is more likely to accept lower wages from the high-status firm. Lenders prefer to lend money to high-status firms because they expect them to repay more readily. This is why

---

[13] Godart, F., A. Shipilov, and K. Claes. 2013. The impact of outward personnel mobility networks on organizational creativity. *Organization Science* 10.

[14] Gulati, R. 1999. Network location and learning: The influence of network resources and firm capabilities on alliance formation. *Strategic Management Journal* 20(5).

[15] Castellucci, F. and G. Ertug. 2010. What's in it for them? Advantages of higher status partners in exchange relationships. *Academy of Management Journal* 53(1): 149–166.

lenders are more likely to agree to high-status firms' requests for lower borrowing costs.[16]

These third-degree advantages come together in a powerful way. For instance, firms with ideas for new products may prefer to launch cooperatively with high-status firms instead of on their own, which gives the high-status firm information, cooperation, and power that would not be available to others.

When Network Status Matters Most

Network status becomes increasingly influential for determining a firm's overall status as uncertainty around actual quality of its product or service increases. When quality is difficult to determine or the consequences of getting quality judgments wrong are high, network status cues become most important. In these situations, operational status based on past performance is more difficult to establish, so it is not reliable. Knowing that a firm has been able to form alliances with other high-status partners provides some confidence that it must be of high quality.

So, think about situations in which quality is difficult to determine. If your customers can't determine your product quality until after purchase, then network status is vital to them. And when it takes a longer period of time after purchase to determine quality, network status matters even more in the customer's calculation. For example, consider how a 35-year-old would make decisions about purchasing investment products intended to secure an active and luxurious retirement 30 years later. It's difficult to determine the quality of the products offered until close to retirement, at which point it is too late. The volatility and the confusing avalanche of information on

---

[16] Podolny, J.M. 1993. A status-based model of market competition. *American Journal of Sociology* 98: 829–872.

competing products make this process even more difficult. However, knowing that others you respect have chosen to work with the same investment professionals or purchase the same products provides comfort—a cue based on relationships. Similarly, when quality uncertainty is high, potential alliance partners make similar inferences about your firm's quality and rely more heavily on your network status.

New firms, which we discuss in more depth in Chapter 9, are often relatively unknown and their success is initially based more on alliances and network status than actual quality. Even if a new entrepreneurial venture has produced high-quality or industry-leading technology, it may never gain a sufficient piece of the market because its quality is difficult to evaluate, and so others use different cues. Producing great products may not be enough.

There are many cases of new technologies that have been heralded as leading-edge innovations but still do not fulfill their potential because innovators and investors are puzzled about how to make money from them. For example, in biotechnology, the process of translating new technology developments into commercialized products is plagued with uncertainty. As a result, investors must rely on other cues to evaluate the quality or commercial potential of biotech innovations. There's a vast body of research showing that investors and others consider who the biotech firm has established alliances with. Alliances with high-status pharmaceutical companies will lead others to judge the innovation and biotech firm as high quality. This often leads to more funding opportunities for the biotech firms.

What High-Status Companies Can Do with Their Status

Which is the highest status company in the world? You won't find the answer to this question on Wikipedia. But, we can

Table 6.1 The world's highest status alliance partners,
2008–2011

Name	Company description	Country
KEPCO	Utility company	Korea
Petroleos de Venezuela	Oil and gas company	Venezuela
RWE AG	Utility company	Germany
Mitsubishi Corporation	Trading company	Japan
Gazprom	Gas company	Russia
Mitsui & Co., Ltd.	Trading company	Japan
ITOCHU Corporation	Trading company	Japan
PETRONAS	Oil and gas company	Malaysia
Mitsubishi Heavy Industries	Shipbuilding and heavy industries company	Japan
Hitachi, Ltd.	Engineering and electronics conglomerate	Japan

answer it using alliance-mapping tools we've developed based on data for over 15,000 firms that announced alliances between 2008 and 2011. Recall that the status of a firm is a function of the status of the firm's partners and that of its partners' partners. So, to answer the question about the highest status company in the world, we need to look not only at which partners each firm has in its alliance portfolio, but also whether the firm's partners have connections to high-status partners of their own. Keep in mind that the size of the firm's alliance portfolio does not fully determine its status. A firm with a few partners in its portfolio might actually have high status if these partners are of high status themselves.

Table 6.1 shows the ranking of the 10 highest status firms in the world according to our research.[17] As it turns out, this

---

[17]Technical details of this analysis are in Appendix One.

Figure 6.2: KEPCO alliance portfolio, second-degree perspective

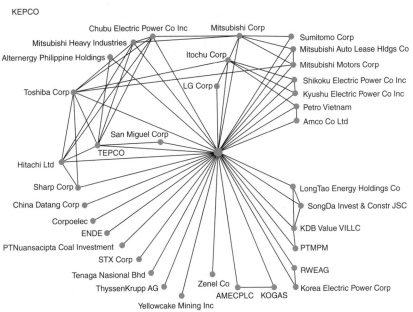

list does not include Google or Microsoft or even Apple. The highest status firm in the world is called Korean Electric Power Corporation (KEPCO). Figure 6.2 shows KEPCO's alliance portfolio and Figure 6.3 depicts its alliance network. KEPCO's number of partners is similar to Samsung's, but KEPCO's partners are much more connected to other firms in their industries, so KEPCO's status is much higher than Samsung's. Samsung belongs to the World's Top 150 companies by status, not to the World's Top 10. Because KEPCO works with many other high-status firms such as Sumitomo Corporation, ThyssenKrupp, Toshiba, and firms from the Mitsubishi keiretsu, such as Mitsubishi Motors and Mitsubishi Heavy Industries, new partners are willing to do business with KEPCO. This allows the company to expand into emerging markets as varied as Vietnam, the

Figure 6.3: KEPCO alliance network, third-degree perspective

Note: some of the firms' names are not indicated on the graph to preserve its readability.

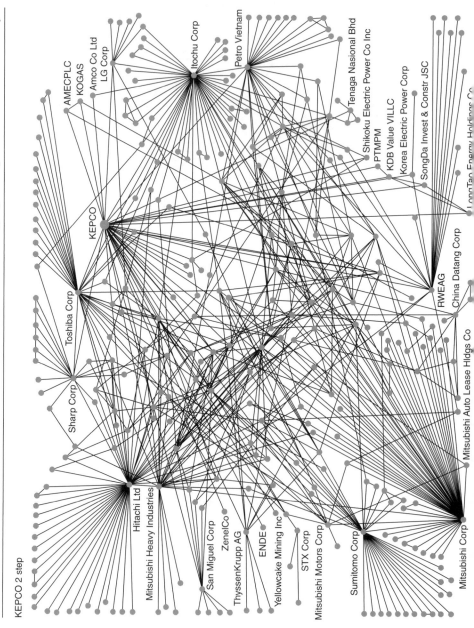

Philippines, United Arab Emirates, and Venezuela. KEPCO's revenues from worldwide activities amounted to a very respectable $39 billion in 2010.[18] As a more general observation, there are many utility companies in our Top 10 list. Because utility and infrastructure projects are highly capital intensive, these firms form many alliances. At the same time, partners in these projects have to be very reliable, respectable, and influential. The costs of failure in a public utility project can be very high and have huge economic and societal repercussions. These costs are immediately clear to the customers, which are governments and their officials who make decisions with an eye to the political costs of failure. This is why customers prefer to work with high-quality and reliable suppliers on these projects. And this is exactly what the concept of a firm's status captures.

High-status firms can be in charge of their alliance networks because they have a greater range of potential partners to choose from than low-status firms have. As a result, a high-status firm has the best chance of achieving network advantage by configuring its alliance portfolio to fit the industry conditions and its strategy. In other words, the high-status firm can construct its second-degree alliance portfolio based on the ideal configuration indicated by the Configuration Alignment Tool (CAT) introduced in Chapter 4. In contrast, a low-status firm will find it more difficult to build its ideal portfolio.

As you recall, in a dynamic industry, firms need to try to maintain dynamic hub-and-spoke portfolios, and high-status firms will be best positioned to accomplish this. For example, the biotechnology industry alliance network has long been characterized by the hub-and-spoke structure. This alliance network is also highly dynamic with many added and dropped ties. At the center of the network, there are the pioneering

---

[18] http://en.wikipedia.org/wiki/Korea_Electric_Power_Corporation.

biotechnology firms that gained status from their early successes: Centocor, Chiron, Amgen, Genentech, and Genzyme. These firms eventually became so valuable for their knowledge, intellectual property, products, and network positions, that many of them were acquired—Centocor by Johnson & Johnson, Chiron by Novartis, Genentech by Roche, and Genzyme by Sanofi. These acquisitions were important for the biotech firms because the acquirers paid a premium for them, and the firms carried on growing their businesses. Amgen, which remained independent, continued to leverage its network to develop new products.

As you know from Chapter 4, in a stable industry, everyone will benefit from building integrated networks, but the biggest beneficiaries will be the high-status firms at the center of the alliance network. High status gives these firms the ability to make decisions that affect not only their direct ties but also their partners' ties. Global liner shipping is an example of such an industry. The high-status firms such as Mitsui O.S.K. Lines (MOL), Nippon Yusen Kaisha (NYK), and Hapag-Lloyd (Hapag) have formed an integrated network of alliances both among each other and including lower status shipping companies. Figure 6.4 shows a picture of the complex network of alliances in the shipping industry. The integration in such a network is important because it allows the players to ensure predictability of shipping schedules and deliveries around the world, which is of paramount importance to their customers. If there is a disruption in any part of this integrated network, such as a natural disaster for example, the shipping companies which are not affected by this disaster can take over the shipments for the companies in the troubled regions, assuring the continued functioning of the global economy.

Public utility firms also compete in an industry that favors an integrated alliance portfolio. This is because firms need to

Figure 6.4: The global liner shipping industry network (1994)

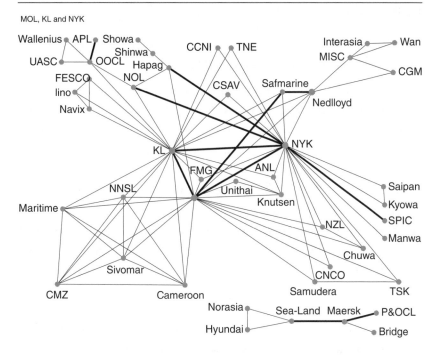

share the capital risks and learn from each other. They do not experience the major technological disruptions seen in the semiconductor or pharmaceutical industries. KEPCO's status allows it to construct a mostly integrated portfolio with partners who work together. Other firms are willing to allow KEPCO to take the lead in the construction of alliances involving partners who work together in other alliances because KEPCO is a high-status partner and firms listen to its opinions. By building an integrated network, KEPCO guarantees for itself the sharing of risks, a steady supply of raw materials, and continuous process improvement through collective learning as well as assistance from its partners when needed. In other words, high status allows KEPCO to build an integrated alliance portfolio and stability of its alliance network becomes the driver for the company's network advantage.

And What About Low-Status Firms?

Low-status firms find it more difficult to construct their alliance portfolios because they have fewer choices of firms that would want to work with them. Some low-status firms can prosper nonetheless if they have at least some connections to the high-status firms by building hub-and-spoke networks that include partners not shared with the high-status firms. In this way low-status firms hope that they can discover new and valuable opportunities from other low-status partners that, in turn, can be combined with their own resources and those of their current high-status collaborators. In other words, even the low-status firms should try to act as brokers of information and as enablers of new ventures. This role is only tolerated as long as they are able to access opportunities that the high-status firms have not noticed and are unable to access on their own. This means that it is very important for the low-status firms to identify and lock in opportunities quickly.

Electromode is a South African music label that was able to enhance its status by partnering with high-status firms. Compared to the big players in the music industry, like Warner and BMG, Electromode is definitely a low-status firm. Faced with the reduction of revenue from the traditional music media of CDs and cassettes and a slow increase in revenues from digital products associated with music (song downloads or artist-branded paraphernalia such as digital wallpaper), Electromode wanted to identify a new business model. The new idea came when the company's owner decided to combine elements that were previously unconnected. He decided to bring together music artists, major consumer goods brands, and companies with social media data-mining expertise. Departing from the traditional sponsorship model, Electromode decided to transform itself into a music advertising agency that heavily relied on social media to reach its audiences. The company capitalized on its knowledge of music tastes in South Africa and used this to approach global consumer goods companies such as Puma and Nestlé. Instead of creating commercials in which artists would explicitly promote a company's product, Electromode suggested that the artists adopt the product as a part of their personal expression in the social media space. They proposed that the positive aura around the artists created by their social media followers would then result in a positive aura about the consumer goods with which the artists associated. To capture the resulting buzz around the product (or the company brand) and provide the client (Nestlé or Puma) with this information to use in determining the return on its marketing spend, Electromode planned to used webdata tracking firms.

Using this business model, "Cone Like a Rock Star" was one of the most successful campaigns produced by Electromode. This campaign involved connecting Lonehill Estate—one of the top-performing South African bands—with Nestlé, the global food and consumer products company based in Switzerland. Nestlé's objective was to promote selling its waffle cone ice cream products. In the summer of 2012, Lonehill Estate agreed to perform in Montreux, Switzerland. Its South African and worldwide fans were asked to make funny web videos where they would "cone like a rock star" (in other words, sing or dance to a band's music with some imagery of a cone around them). The fans also voted for the best videos, whose authors were invited to accompany the band to its concert in Switzerland. The campaign generated lots of videos that indirectly promoted Nestlé's products, including people dancing with the highway yellow cones on their heads, having their faces poked with ice cream cones, and so on. Many of them were posted on the Facebook page "Yes, We Cone [With Nestlé King

Cone]"[19] and the band itself posted heavily-followed videos about its stay in Switzerland.[20] After the trip, the "Yes, We Cone" page was transformed into the Nestlé fan-club community and the web data analysis firm provided Nestlé with research showing how the brand's positive visibility and buzz from the fans increased. Essentially, Electromode became the hub in the portfolio and the artists, consumer goods companies, and web data analysis companies became the spokes. Despite Electromode's low status, its deep relationships with South African artists made it an attractive partner for Nestlé, a high-status firm. Electromode was also able to use its relationships with the web data analysis companies to show global consumer brands their return on investment.

Nestlé was willing to partner with Electromode because it realized that low-status firms are a big source of disruptive innovations. To learn new tricks, high-status firms need to have some low-status firms in their portfolios to make sure that they are not shut off from these innovations. Firms in the pharmaceutical industry understand the need to partner both with low- and high-status firms very well. Genentech, one of the pioneers in the biotechnology industry, had alliances with lower status firms such as BioInvent (development and commercialization of cardiovascular drugs),[21] but also with high-status institutes and organizations like the National Institutes of Health, Eastman Kodak (film and chemicals), Eli Lilly (pharmaceuticals), and Boehringer Ingelheim (pharmaceuticals). Over time, Genentech came to occupy a high-status position in the pharmaceutical industry, but it never gave up its low-status partner affiliations. It knew that in this industry existing knowledge

---

[19] http://www.facebook.com/YesWeCone.

[20] http://lonehillestate.wordpress.com/2012/07/08/performing-at -montreux/.

[21] http://www.bioinvent.se/partners.aspx.

will quickly become obsolete and current research may be on the wrong track, so high-status partners cannot be the sole source of long-term value. As Genentech's network kept growing, one of its partners, the pharmaceutical firm Hoffman-La Roche, acquired it for $46.8 billion.[22]

Going Forward

Now that you know that status is valuable, you will want to understand how your firm can achieve third-degree network advantage by using status. In the next chapter, we will discuss how to visualize your firm's status and what you can do to protect and expand this valuable asset.

Chapter Highlights

• Status is the perceived level of leadership and influence a firm has in its industry. It has two components: operational status and network status. Your firm's operational status depends on the quality of your products and on the strength of your brand. Your network status depends on the leadership and influence of your partners.

• Status especially matters when a customer cannot objectively evaluate the quality of your firm's product before buying it.

• The higher your status, the easier it is to construct your alliance portfolio according to the structure indicated by the Configuration Alignment Tool (CAT).

• Low-status firms can benefit from building a hub-and-spoke network in which they connect high-status firms to other lower status firms.

• High-status firms will benefit from having a small number of low-status firms in their alliance portfolios because the low-status firms can be sources of innovative ideas.

---

[22] http://en.wikipedia.org/wiki/Genentech.

CHAPTER SEVEN

ASSESSING AND INCREASING YOUR STATUS: EXTRACTING ENERGY FROM WAVES

Kai Bergman, founder of the Finnish start-up AppMall, had a grand vision.[1] He created this company in 2008 to battle Apple and Google in the market for mobile applications, which at that time was estimated at $10 billion globally, with an expected 100% annual growth by 2011. This was a great market for Apple and Google, but not for telecom operators. Most of the content provided through Apple and Google was (and still is) in English, a foreign language for many customers outside the U.S., Canada, the U.K., and Australia. Kai wanted to create a service to help mobile operators set up "white label portals," in other words their own branded "app" stores. This way, the telecom operators, not Apple or Google, would own the relationships with the consumers who bought apps. He expected strong demand in emerging markets where this platform could provide local developers with an opportunity to sell their apps to the local populations in local languages. Between 2008 and 2011, Kai

---

[1] Some names and geographical references in this case are disguised to preserve confidentiality.

succeeded in attracting the early round of funding for his venture and employed 20 people in the company's Helsinki headquarters. He also created an excellent back office in India with another 18 employees to write code for the platform. Yet, in 2012, the company filed for bankruptcy; it couldn't win a single contract from a major telecom operator.

At the same time, Floating Power Plant (FPP), a start-up from Denmark, was realizing its own great dream. Since 2004, the company had been working on a prototype for an offshore platform called "Poseidon" that would convert the energy of waves and wind into electricity.[2] According to FPP documents, in 2012, the inherent energy in waves was 1,000 times greater than that of wind and the estimated market value for wave energy was around $500 billion. Poseidon-type platforms could be put into operation on Europe's Atlantic coast, in Australia, and on the West Coast of the U.S. Despite employing only four people, FPP managed to build and test a fully functioning prototype of the power plant. It also received several rounds of financing. After eight years in operation, the company had a product it was ready to market. Then, it looked for partners to invest in building its network of energy wave converters.

Although FPP had yet to turn a profit in 2013 as we were writing this book, the firm has outlasted AppMall and was able to secure significantly more financing. Despite its smaller number of employees, FPP was able to build a technology that was much more capital intensive than AppMall's. While FPP may obviously encounter difficulties going forward, its early success can be explained by how it built its alliance portfolio. From the early days, FPP developed its technology in collaboration with three high-status partners (see Table 7.1).

The glue that held this network together was the patented "integrating" technology FPP developed to connect the different

---

[2] http://www.floatingpowerplant.com/.

Table 7.1 FPP's partners

Partner	Partner contribution
Siemens	Expertise in power generators
Fritz Schur Energy	Knowledge about making hydraulic pumps
Knud Hansen	Architectural solutions

elements resulting from its individual relationships with these partners.[3]

FPP increased its own status in the eyes of investors and sought to do so in the eyes of the customers by "borrowing" status from the firms it worked with. Since neither investors nor customers could judge the quality of FPP's product, they had to rely on "signals" sent from FPP's alliance portfolio. FPP hoped that investors and customers would believe that if this firm was working with Siemens, Knud Hansen, and Fritz Schur Energy, all high-status players in their respective industries, then FPP's own status must be higher than that of other start-ups in the same industry.

In contrast, AppMall did not build any alliances with high-status firms. It tried to access foreign markets from its head office in Helsinki and it did not closely collaborate with any well-known telecom operator in developing its products. It also did not team up with any partners to build political connections in the countries where it planned to market its services. In short, when AppMall offered its services, it had neither status of its own nor could it borrow status from any of its partners.

In Chapter 6, we discussed the two main sources of status: operational status achieved by emphasizing the value of the company's products and services and network status gained by partnering with high-status partners. We also suggested that

---

[3] http://www.floatingpowerplant.com/?pageid=332.

companies need to rely on public relations strategies to support both sources of status. In this chapter, we introduce an exercise to help you:

- compare your firm's status to the status of other firms in your industry;
- identify partners you could collaborate with to enhance your status.

We also recommend specific steps your firm can take to become attractive to high-status partners using strategic public relations. In other words, we show you how to avoid making AppMall's mistakes. Instead, you will be able to extract third-degree network advantage from your industry just as FPP extracted energy from the ocean. Through your status, you will make waves.

Understanding and Enhancing Your Firm's Status

How can *your* firm evaluate and build its status? To help you answer this question we developed the Third-Degree Assessment Tool, which is included in the Toolbox, Appendix Two. This chapter covers the work involved with completing this tool. Rest assured that you don't need to have an alliance network picture for your industry in order to succeed at this exercise. The analysis is quite straightforward using the steps summarized in Figure 7.1 and briefly discussed in the following sections.

Step 1: Identify High-Status Firms

To begin this analysis, answer the following question: What firms in your industry command influence and respect from others? Try to identify up to 10 names. These are the high-status firms.

Figure 7.1: Steps in the Third-Degree Assessment Tool

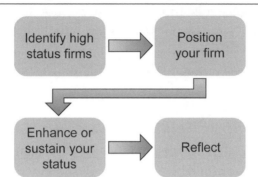

To do this systematically, the easiest place to start is by thinking about your direct competitors. Then, expand your search to suppliers, buyers, or makers of complementary products or services. Once you've identified these firms, rank them based on your *perception* of their influence and respect.

Verify your analysis by taking an outside perspective. That is, if you asked your competitors, customers, and suppliers the same question about the names of respected and influential firms in your industry, would they identify the same firms and rank the firms the same way you did?

Step 2: Position Your Firm

Next, ask the question: Does your firm belong to this list of influential and respected firms? A brutally honest answer will help you understand whether your firm has high status. If your firm isn't among the Top 10 high-status names that others would mention, then it's probably not of high status.

Does your firm have alliances with any of the high-status firms? If your firm is both high status and it has alliances with these partners, then your high-status position is very solid. If your firm has alliances with these high-status partners, but it doesn't make the Top 10 list, then this is still good news: you are "borrowing" status from your high-status partners. If you are not a high-status firm and you do not have high-status partners, then your business risks eventually going down the path of AppMall unless you work on increasing both your network and operational status.

Step 3: Enhance or Sustain Your Status

How can you increase the number of high-status partners in your alliance portfolio?

A communications consultant who has worked with major pharmaceutical companies once confidentially told us that "money is not enough to build status, and you cannot build status from nothing." This means that you can't buy status if you don't have a credible product, service, technology, or capability to back up your communications. If you do have this strong foundation, amplify its power through communication so that others notice and the high quality becomes a part of your firm's attractiveness to other partners.

Here's an example from the fashion goods industry. LVMH benefits from the longstanding tradition of French quality products and it has many industry awards to show for its own record of high quality. LVMH doesn't shy away from telling customers about the quality of its products. It buys the most expensive advertising space in the major publications read by their target market segment, such as the *New York Times*. It hires top fashion models to exhibit LVMH products during fashion shows and uses well-known personalities such as Muhammad Ali, Mikhail Gorbachev, and Michael Phelps to advertise its travel accessories. This approach helps increase awareness of the company's brand, and together with the quality of the company's products, it constructs the foundation on which status can be further developed.

Using Public Relations Strategies to Increase Your Status

Beyond spending money on advertising, in this next section we discuss five public relations strategies you can use to increase your status:

- Take a leadership role in industry events.
- Develop a communication strategy around the critical industry issue.
- Become the convener of industry events.
- Announce small wins with alliance partners.
- Become a thought leader on alliances and beyond.

Take a Leadership Role in Industry Events

How can your company project a high status? This can be done through strategically managing the company's participation in industry events such as conferences, seminars, exhibitions, or round tables that bring together senior decision makers, media, and other stakeholders. To project a higher status, ask your executives to regularly attend and become members of the leadership team that organizes these events. In fact, it's very important to make attending and helping organize these events a part of their job descriptions. The audience expects important people to be on stage during these events. If your people are on stage, then the company that employs them must be of high status. It's often the case that membership in the organizing committees is linked to the level of sponsorship a company is willing to provide. Encourage your company to buy the highest sponsorship level it can possibly afford. In addition to including your team members in the organizing committee, try to attract visibility by displaying a larger logo or obtaining a bigger exhibition booth at conferences. It sounds simple, but attendees tend to equate these things with the status of your organization.

Industries also create task forces, composed of executives from different companies, formed to agree on common standards, to research future trends, or to collectively communicate with important stakeholders such as governments or consumer associations. Make sure your employees take leadership roles in these task forces. A recent study that examined standard setting in the telecommunications industry found that the firms with a greater number of employees participating in the industry's standard-setting task forces on a regular basis had more influence in setting the industry's standards.[4] Because participation in these task forces is voluntary, many companies tend to shy away from them. They are actually powerful mechanisms for enhancing influence, reputation, and, by extension, status.

Develop a Communication Strategy around the Critical Industry Issue

Companies within an industry often face a critical and shared issue such as sustainability for the oil and gas industry, supply-chain responsibility for manufacturing firms, or affordability of medicines for the pharmaceutical industry. Identify the critical issue for your industry and build your firm's communication strategy around it. When you do, you send the message that you understand what's going on and serve as a valuable source of ideas and support. Because these issues are often delicate, consider securing professional help from communications specialists so that you can demonstrate your leadership responsibly and effectively. They can help you with media training for your executives, writing editorials and commentaries, putting together presentations, and identifying the channels through which this content is made public.

---

[4]Dokko, G. and L. Rosenkopf. 2010. Social capital for hire? Mobility of technical professionals and firm influence in wireless standards committees. *Organizational Science* 21(3): 677–695.

The issue-related content should emphasize the unique contributions that your company is making to the advancement of thinking about the issue. These contributions could be based on the unique technologies, expertise, or market presence that you have. For example, Roger Martin, former Dean of the Rotman School of Management at the University of Toronto, has spearheaded the school's drive to incorporate integrative thinking into its programs. The Rotman School believes that the MBA curriculum has become so fractured along individual functions (e.g. strategy, finance, marketing) that students can excel in each one of them without seeing how businesses make connections across these disciplines. Roger Martin's approach generated a lot of external publicity for the Rotman School and allowed its faculty to showcase its expertise in cross-disciplinary thinking. Because many professors from the Harvard Business School (HBS) were also interested in this topic, the Rotman School enhanced its status by inviting HBS professors to its events. Leading management thinkers, like Peter Drucker, have also criticized the lack of integrative thinking in the traditional MBA curriculum. Roger Martin invited them to the Rotman School events as well, and this further enhanced its status.

Become the Convener of Industry Events

As you become better known in your industry, you'll be able to organize events on your own. For example, companies such as Pfizer and Johnson & Johnson in the pharmaceutical industry are well known for convening industry events where they bring together their suppliers and partners as well as other stakeholders such as doctors, insurance company representatives, or even government officials. As a convener, you get the prime spot at your own event and your executives can be on stage as much of the time as you want. Organizing such events shows others that you know the important people in your industry and that they need to know you if they want to get access to your event.

Here's what you need to do to organize an industry event:

- Choose a compelling and relevant topic—perhaps one related to the critical industry issue or to an emerging technology or market.
- Secure attendance by a handful of high-status participants that you might know through your personal network.
- Use the "borrowed" status of these high-status participants to attract others on your exclusive invitation list.
- Convey your confidence by announcing that you will make this a regular event. Then, by running this event several times you can ensure a continuous improvement in your reputation— ergo your status—and your influence in the industry.

Announce Small Wins with Alliance Partners

Let's say your efforts paid off and a high-status company returned your phone calls, you progressed through negotiation, and now you have an alliance partner. It goes without saying that if your customers, suppliers, or competitors know who your high-status partners are, they will think better of you. When should you announce this good news? Many companies rush to announce their alliances before the ink dries on the signed contracts. However, as you know, many alliances fail and alliances with high-status partners tend to fail more spectacularly, especially for the low-status partners. If you're a low-status firm and your alliance with a high-status partner dissolves within three months, an early announcement could do a great deal of harm. You risk having other firms think of you as an unreliable partner even though this might not be true. Why? High-status firms are always thought to be reliable partners, so it's usually their partners who take the blame for a failed alliance—even if they performed well.

The exact timing of your communication will depend on how soon you can generate early alliance successes, also known as "quick wins" from collaboration. These are important in any alliance as a way of building trust between the partners. A quick win could be the creation of a product prototype, completion of a small part of a technology transfer, the culmination of a joint market research initiative, or winning your first contract together. Even if this accomplishment is very small compared to the initial scope of the alliance, the fact that you arrived at it together with your partner is an important element that's going to help your alliance going forward.

As soon as you get a quick win, communicate it to the public. It's better if this communication comes from both partners—that is via an article, media event, or even a blog post that involves participants from both firms—so that the world will know what a great partner you are.

Become a Thought Leader on Alliances and Beyond

There's no better way to project your company's status than to get someone else whose opinion is credible to write about you. While companies always think about business journalists as the sources of such writing, top business schools can also be great places for you to develop and project thought leadership. Think about how positively you perceive the role model companies and people you've read about in this and previous business books.

Professional business educators like us are always looking for interesting examples to use in our classrooms. How do you introduce your story to people who are writing articles (and even books), teaching scores of people interested in business, and, very importantly, talking with credibility to opinion leaders? Try to get engaged with business researchers and teachers. For example, you could arrange for some of your executives to give guest lectures in courses where the subject matter is close to their areas of expertise. Attending academic conferences, like those run by the Strategic Management

Society,[5] is a great place to meet business school professors. If you can develop relationships with us (and academics in general) and convince us that you have an interesting story to tell, we may write a case study about you and then you become a "classroom" if not a "household" name. Better still, you could be invited to present at networking events that business schools organize for other executives, MBA students, or alumni.

Take, for example, Steve Steinhilber, Vice President of Cisco Systems, who is a protagonist in at least one Harvard Business School case study on strategic alliances. He presented his thoughts on managing strategic alliances at Stanford Executive Briefings and also wrote a book on strategic alliance management at Cisco with Harvard Business School Press. He's seen as one of the top practitioner thought leaders in this domain. Companies from other industries even started to invite Cisco's executives to speak at their events in order to share their alliance management knowledge.[6]

In Europe, John Bell, the Head of Strategy and Partnerships at Philips Electronics, routinely participates as a speaker in the Strategic Management Society conference. He also teaches short sessions in the INSEAD program on Managing Partnerships and Strategic Alliances. This exposes him to a broad executive audience, including readers like you (his experiences are also discussed in Chapter 10).

These examples describe people projecting their companies' expertise in managing alliances, but you don't have to focus your energies in that area only. Which topics would you like your firm to be known and respected for in the industry community? These topics could include knowledge about markets you entered or the technologies you're working on. What have

---

[5] http://strategicmanagement.net/conf/index.php.
[6] http://www.amanet.org/training/articles/Ciscos-Perspective-on -Strategic-Alliances.aspx.

you learned from something you've tried or done that you're willing to share with others? Could you co-write a white paper and circulate it to your partners and prospective partners? How could you collaborate with a university or a business school to publicize your knowledge? Of course, you don't want to disclose sensitive information. But if your company has expertise in an area, there's a lot you can share with non-experts without disclosing your trade secrets.

Be Prepared for Greater Scrutiny and Commit Long Term

As you're building your status, be aware that this is not only a source of opportunity but also a source of risk. One automotive industry study showed that the higher the reputation of the car company, the more this reputation suffers as a result of product recalls.[7] People expect good judgment from high-status firms and stories about a high-status firm's "fall from grace" attract media attention. In some cases a high-status firm might attract unwanted attention because of the things that its partners do. For example, when L'Oréal purchased The Body Shop, it attracted threats from animal rights groups to boycott The Body Shop's products. This happened because L'Oréal's practice of testing products on animals directly conflicted with The Body Shop's established status and reputation as a supporter of ethical consumerism and protector of animal rights.[8]

In a similar example, French President François Hollande was elected in 2012 on a populist platform best summarized by

---

[7] Rhee, M. and P.R. Haunschild. 2006. The liability of good reputation: A study of product recalls in the U.S. automobile industry. *Organizational Science* 17(1): 101–117.

[8] http://www.guardian.co.uk/business/2006/mar/17/retail .animalrights.

his 2008 statement "I don't like the rich."[9] Upon winning a hotly contested election from Nicolas Sarkozy, whom Hollande accused of spending too much time with the "rich," President Hollande selected Jérôme Cahuzac to be the Budget Minister. Cahuzac is a former cosmetic surgeon who turned a socialist politician in 1997. President Hollande's status (and approval ratings) sunk after it became known that for 20 years Mr Cahuzac had maintained an undisclosed Swiss bank account (which was later moved to Singapore) in which he hid over 600,000 euros and that he lied to the Parliament about having this account.[10] Bottom line, as you build your status, be prepared to deal with the consequences of greater scrutiny, especially if something goes wrong with you or those around you.

All of the steps outlined in the Third-Degree Assessment Tool will work best and will reinforce each other if you have a long-term commitment to building your status. That commitment begins with the last step in the tool, Step 4: Reflection. Be sure to take time to identify three key actions you plan to take to increase your status and work your plan. For example, if you decide to become a spokesperson for a critical industry issue, once you've identified it, stay committed to it, and take credible actions to move it forward. Securing leadership roles in industry events requires long-term planning at least a year in advance. Organizing your own conference might take anywhere from 12 to 18 months of work. And it may take a while to generate even "quick wins" worthy of a communication.

More importantly, know that building alliances takes time and you'll have ups and downs. When you remain committed, you demonstrate the long-term perspective associated with high-status firms. Obviously, developing a track record for being a

---

[9] http://fr.wikiquote.org/wiki/Fran%C3%A7ois_Hollande.

[10] http://www.guardian.co.uk/world/2013/apr/02/jerome-cahuzac -france-offshore-account?INTCMP=SRCH.

good alliance partner is a long exercise. But, remember that status is a durable source of network advantage, and once you build status, it becomes difficult for others to replicate.

The Birth of Poseidon

Let's return to the opening story of this chapter. Even though executives working for FPP did not use the tool we outlined, they could not have created the Poseidon platform without intuitively understanding the need to increase their firm's status. Their company was a start-up that had limited resources. You can imagine that they began by asking themselves who were the high-status firms in marine engineering. And, of course, the names of firms such as Siemens, Fritz Schur Energy, and Knud Hansen came up. All of these companies were developing plans to enter the renewable energy market. So strategy fit between FPP and the high-status partners was there.

How did they get "in" with these firms? Initially, FPP approached them as a buyer of their products or services using the funding it received from the venture capitalists. In addition, FPP had developed a patented "integrating" technology for combining different technologies from different partners. High-status companies quickly understood the potential of this FPP technology. They agreed to work with FPP not simply as a buyer of their services, but as a partner with which they shared their knowledge, hoping to learn new things in return. This resulted in a resource fit: instead of simply paying the partners for their products and services, FPP was also providing them with opportunities to learn about new applications of their expertise. Clearly, this small start-up had a different organization structure than the large multinational firms, so FPP had to learn how to deal with large organizations. This task was made easier by the fact that the FPP board members who were heavily involved with company operations also had extensive experience working with large firms. Culture fit was there as well because all the major partners participated in this project through their Danish subsidiaries, so the alliance partners did not have to overcome barriers based on cultural values. Fortunately, the organizational cultures of FPP and its partners were also similar, as all of them were firms with entrepreneurial spirit focusing on solving complex engineering tasks.

In addition to making these alliances, FPP's executives participated extensively in industry events. For example, CEO Anders Køhler has been a speaker, participant, and exhibitor at the Envirotech summit in the U.K. since 2011. He announced the debut of construction on the Poseidon prototype at this event.[11] This conference earned FPP good publicity because many venture capital firms as well as other key players in the green technology industry attended the conference. As FPP attracts new partners, it communicates about these alliance relationships. FPP's website now features a presentation of the company's technology as well as the list of its alliance partners.

In short, had it not been for the company's strategy of building alliances with high-status firms, Poseidon would not have been born.

Going Forward

In the next chapter, we'll integrate the insights you've gained from using the first-, second-, and third-degree perspectives to increase your own firm's network advantage. We'll explore how your company's status determines the strategy for your overall alliance portfolio. That is, it helps you decide whether to build a new alliance portfolio on your own (based on the first- and

---

[11] http://www.greentechmedia.com/events/live/nordic-green-ii/speakers.

second-degree analysis you conducted using the tools introduced in earlier chapters) or to join alliance portfolios built by other firms.

Chapter Highlights

- The Third-Degree Assessment Tool helps you identify the high-status players in your industry, determine the status of your company, and think through the ways you can enhance your own network status.
- You can build your status strategically using public relations. There are five ways to increase awareness of your firm:
  - take a leadership role in industry events
  - develop a communication strategy around the critical industry issue
  - become the convener of events
  - announce small wins with alliance partners
  - become the industry's thought leaders.
- Building status is not a short-term act; it requires long-term commitment of resources and attention from your company's executives. Be prepared to handle the greater scrutiny conferred by high status as well as the greater benefits and rewards.

CHAPTER EIGHT

MAXIMIZING NETWORK ADVANTAGE: DESIGNING YOUR ALLIANCE PORTFOLIO STRATEGY

Biocon holds the distinction of being India's oldest and most prominent biotech company. Founded in 1978 by Kiran Mazumdar-Shaw, Biocon sells biotechnology products based on advanced fermentation technology; it employed more than 6,900 people in 2012, and generated 2012 revenues of approximately $446 million (25.4 billion rupees). Biocon spent a long time selling its products to developed-market companies. However, even after it proved its technological leadership through a unique patented process, the company could not easily form alliances. One possible explanation for other firms' reluctance to work with Biocon may have been its location in India where some local pharmaceutical firms reverse-engineer and produce drugs that are under patent in the major developed nations in order to sell them in nations where those patents are not honored. Or, perhaps the major pharmaceutical firms just preferred working with developed-nation alliance partners. It's also highly likely that, in the beginning, Biocon experienced problems forming alliances because it was a new and unproven firm in the eyes of potential alliance partners. New firms in the developed world face this problem too.

How did Biocon get to where it is now from such a weak start? Biocon took steps to solve the reverse-engineering concern by forming Syngene, a separate contract research subsidiary which started developing a set of outsourcing relationships with major pharmaceutical firms while Biocon continued developing its main business. The success of Syngene's contract research convinced other pharmaceutical firms that Biocon and Syngene were serious alliance partners. Biocon also made clear that it developed its own products without any knowledge gained from Syngene in making its products. After establishing this track record and the unique value it could bring to partnerships, Biocon could start research and development collaborations in its core businesses. It now has a string of collaborations with partners such as Mylan, Abbott, DuPont, and Pfizer. Biocon's capabilities and intentions were simply underestimated, and it needed to prove itself before it could be treated as an equal partner.

Biocon's early days were similar to those of a town that lacked road connections. It could still prosper to some extent with its local businesses, but it lacked the benefits of information, trade links, and influence. Many towns in Roman Britannia were like this. We know that Londinium developed through its position in the center of the road network. Clearly, there were advantages to being connected. For a road-less town, the obvious question was how to get a road connection and, because roads were expensive to build, where to connect. The nearest town was not necessarily the answer. Instead, the right answer was to find a road connection that gave the town a well-connected place on the map.

Designing Your Alliance Portfolio

Firms face the same problem: how to enhance their position by connecting to the right partners. So far, you've seen how a firm's alliance portfolio can provide network advantage by providing it with information and cooperation from its partners and with power to influence events. You also saw how a firm can structure its alliance portfolio depending on industry conditions and the firm's goals. The tools we've introduced so far help you understand what an *ideal* alliance portfolio should look like. Now it's time to turn to the real-world task of how to get to the ideal alliance portfolio. One obvious barrier is that alliances are like social dances—there may be some people you'd want to dance with but unless they want to dance with you it's not going to happen. And often competition is the reason they don't want to dance with you: they have eyes for someone else. Like the unpopular kids at school, many firms are left without a partner or stuck with a different partner than they would have liked.

Designing your alliance portfolio is complex because it calls for looking realistically at how attractive your firm is to others and adapting to your limitations. If you're seen as the ideal partner, then you can easily build the ideal alliance portfolio by picking exactly the partners you want. If you're not well known or not seen as the most valuable partner, you have fewer options. Even with fewer options available, there are still choices to make. There are also opportunities to build your status in order to expand your options. Designing your alliance portfolio involves knowing what options are available, choosing among them, and taking actions to expand your future options. In this chapter, we help you determine a realistic strategy for designing your alliance portfolio, even if you're not in an ideal position now. If possible, you should try to build your own alliance portfolio according to the design principles we discussed in Chapters 4 and 5.

Should I Build or Should I Join?

In order to have the freedom to build your own portfolio, two conditions determine whether your firm is appealing enough

Figure 8.1: Steps in the Build or Join Tool

to partner with other firms. Your firm needs autonomy in its industry and attractiveness as a partner. We developed the Build or Join Tool, which you'll find in the Toolbox, Appendix Two, to help you distinguish between your firm's *autonomy* and its *attractiveness*. Figure 8.1 shows the steps you need to take in using this tool.

Step 1: Assess the Autonomy and Attractiveness of Your Firm

In this first step you assess your firm's autonomy in the industry and attractiveness to other firms as a potential partner. These assessments shape your options for designing your portfolio strategy.

- *Autonomy* refers to how much independence a firm has to make its own decisions about how to configure exchange flows within the industry: who does what and how the work is divided up. Autonomous firms have more freedom to build alliance portfolios because they can orchestrate how different firms work together in order to produce a final product or service.
- *Attractiveness* refers to how sought after the firm is as a partner based on its overall status, its clearly formulated vision for an alliance portfolio, or its established track record as a good partner. Attractive partners will more often find that their offers to collaborate get accepted.

Assess Autonomy

Autonomy comes from two characteristics: *uniqueness* and *brokerage position in the industry*. Uniqueness and autonomy go hand in hand because a firm with a unique offering can make the case to potential partners and customers that there is nothing comparable around, so there cannot be any price wars or auctions over what the firm has to offer. For example, Biocon had unique fermentation processes that were valuable to its partners. Also, in the three-way alliance between INSEAD, NES, and Sberbank (discussed in Chapter 5), INSEAD in cooperation with NES offers a unique executive education program for Sberbank. INSEAD had enough Russian-speaking professors to staff most of the core functional courses in the program's curriculum and NES was attractive because it had enough Russian-speaking faculty to staff the courses that INSEAD could not. No other top business school in the world was able to offer such a program. To assess the uniqueness of your firm's product or service, use the diagnostic questions listed under "Uniqueness" in the box below.

Some firms have a role in the industry that makes them a broker of information that can create value. Often the firm with the most information about the customer can create value, but it can also be the firm that integrates technologies, or components, or complex services. When people download games to play on their smartphones, they become customers of the mobile gaming industry, which is a complex set of alliances between game producers, game publishers, platform (programming language) makers, handset makers, and telecommunications carriers. In this industry, brokerage is determined by the collection of information about customer behavior. Early on, telecommunications carriers proved to be dependent on others to undertake this role, which initially left brokerage to game publishers and later on to application stores operated by handset makers. Therefore, uniqueness may be based not only on the unique product or service but also on having a position in the industry that is difficult for the others to imitate.

To assess your firm's brokerage position in the industry, use the diagnostic questions listed under "Brokerage position" in the box below.

Autonomy Diagnostic Questions

Uniqueness
- Do you have few or no close competitors for your product or service?
- When you launch a new product, does it take a long time for a competing product to be introduced?
- If you do not have a close competitor, do significant barriers exist that prevent others from imitating your product or service?

If you answer, "yes" to most or all of these questions, then your firm has high uniqueness.

Brokerage position
- Is your position in the industry one that has an interface with the customer and collects information on the customer?
- Is your position in the industry one that integrates components, technologies, activities, or services?

If you answer, "yes" to one or both of these questions, then your firm performs a brokerage function.

When your firm has either uniqueness or a brokerage function, then, good news, your firm has autonomy.

Assess Attractiveness

We introduced the concept of attractiveness in Chapters 6 and 7. If your firm has high status, others will be attracted by you and want to become your partners. Even firms with low status can overcome this disadvantage under the right circumstances. One way for a low-status firm, such as an entrepreneurial start-up or a firm from an emerging market, to gain attractiveness is to have a clear vision for its alliance portfolio and communicate this vision to potential partners.

In video gaming, Ubisoft, a French video game publisher, presented such a vision and gained the collaboration of Electronic Arts (still one of the top game publishers) and Sierra On-Line (now defunct). In 1986, Electronic Arts and Sierra On-Line were established video game publishers while Ubisoft was a small firm without publishing capability. The key element of Ubisoft's vision at the time was to provide the English language game publishers with access to the growing French video gaming market. As a distributor of video games, Ubisoft was strongly dependent on close collaboration with the publishers. Once Ubisoft secured that collaboration, it made sense for the firm to broaden its alliance network to start developing its own games, which led to the creation of such successful franchises as Rayman and Assassin's Creed. In 2011, Ubisoft was ranked number six for the quality of its video games.[1]

Attractiveness is also high if your firm has the network status that comes from being a good alliance partner. Remember that your network status is created by the status of your alliance partners and your track record of producing good outcomes for partners. The status you get from connecting with high-status partners is based on a perception of quality and

---

[1] http://en.wikipedia.org/wiki/Video_game_publisher.

success; it means that others will see you as important because major firms see you as important. But network status is not directly backed by concrete results, so it can easily be spoiled by a bad alliance outcome or by withdrawal of the high-status partners. Your track record may be less widely known because people have to be familiar with your firm to gauge it, but it's potentially more stable than the connections to other high-status partners who might withdraw or lose status for reasons outside of your control. What's important is that you can influence your network status by delivering successful alliances, and you can increase it by leveraging your successful alliances to gain additional partners.

Use the diagnostic questions in the following box to assess your firm's attractiveness.

Attractiveness Diagnostic Questions

High status
- Does your firm have high status?

Clear vision
- Can you articulate a vision for the alliance portfolio including clear explanations of the roles for each partner, how they contribute value, how they will benefit from their contribution?

If you answer, "yes" to one or both of these questions, then your firm has high attractiveness.

Step 2: Find Your Position in the Matrix

After you assess your autonomy and attractiveness, then you can position your firm in the matrix of options shown in Figure 8.2. If both your autonomy and attractiveness are high, your

Figure 8.2: Build or Join Tool matrix

		Autonomy	
		Low	High
Attractiveness	Low	#1 – Improve autonomy or attractiveness	#2 – Build attractiveness
	High	#3 – Join an alliance portfolio	#4 – Build an alliance portfolio

conclusion is clear: you're free to build an alliance portfolio—position #4 in the matrix. You occupy a position in the industry that gives you the freedom to design how firms work together and to secure the partners you want. This is what INSEAD has done in its three-way alliance with NES and Sberbank.

If your autonomy is low and your attractiveness is high, you will not be able to build an alliance network around your firm. In this case, you cannot design how firms work together in the industry, and you're better off taking a specialized role in an existing alliance network—position #3. Ubisoft adopted this strategy in the 1980s and 1990s. However, once it developed its game-publishing capabilities, Ubisoft's autonomy increased and it was able to build its own alliance networks starting from the mid-1990s to the present time.

What about the last two boxes in the matrix? If you're high on autonomy and low on attractiveness, you need to build your network status by consolidating a track record of being a good alliance partner and/or by formulating a clear vision for an alliance network—position #2. Even though your first collaborations might involve lower status partners, everyone needs to prove themselves in some way. This was the strategy pursued by the Floating Power Plant (FPP) which we discussed in Chapter 7. FPP had the unique technology of converting the energy of waves into electrical power, but as a start-up it was not an attractive partner. Through initial collaborations with smaller players, like Contec, a consulting company, FPP developed a track record of being a good partner. It then asked Contec for referrals to higher status partners like Siemens.

Finally, if you're low in autonomy and attractiveness, you need to improve on at least one dimension before working with others—position #1. Alliances can help you build on your strengths, but they cannot help you overcome this double weakness. AppMall fell into this category (see Chapter 7 for this discussion). Unfortunately, AppMall was able to develop neither autonomy nor attractiveness, so it could not form any meaningful alliances and failed as a result.

Building and Configuring Your Alliance Portfolio

If you're high on autonomy and attractiveness, you can build an alliance portfolio around your firm. The final goal is an alliance portfolio configuration (hub-and-spoke, hybrid, or integrated) which is appropriate for your industry conditions and your goals as suggested by the CAT (see Chapter 5). Even if your final goal is clear, there are many possible paths to take. Should your firm take a stepwise approach of initiating one alliance at a time, or should it form many alliances at once? What is the right sequence for forming the alliances? Which alliance partners are most important?

Although some firms are able to build portfolios very quickly for a specific purpose, such rapid alliance portfolio building is typically the privilege of very high-status firms that are creating a new portfolio for a specific purpose. The classic example is the syndicates used by investment banks to "place" (sell) a firm's securities. These are large short-term alliances with many investment banks that commit to selling the securities to their customers, and they exist only for as long as it takes to sell the securities. When high-status investment banks manage these alliances, the syndicates are very easy to form. Joining them is based on trust; the investment banks do limited checking on the firm and the security, and they rarely fail to place the securities as planned. When there are problems, such as when a Citibank analyst released negative information about the Facebook Initial Public Offering that the bank was backing, everyone takes notice because these negative information spills from inside the syndicates are very unusual.

Most firms do not have the star power that allows for the creation of such instant alliance portfolios, and they do not ask for commitments over such a limited time. Instead, they are lower status firms asking for longer time commitments. They have to overcome much more skepticism. If you're one of these companies, creating an alliance portfolio becomes a step-by-step process, done one alliance at a time. The first partners are important because they will be your deepest collaborators; they will be used to build your network status through being a good partner who adds value; and they will be the "attractors" that bring other alliance partners into your alliance network.

These initial partners should be the ones that create the greatest value in your alliance portfolio. This makes the initial partner selection especially important because these partners are the core of your business and should be stars on compatibility and complementarity in order to ensure high-value collaborations. You use these alliances to establish the track record that becomes the network status that attracts later alliance partners. Later alliance partners look at the overall value of the alliance portfolio, and they're less harsh judges of your firm than the first partners because they assess the entire portfolio, not just your firm. They're also less sensitive to the success of each alliance than those who enter after the initial few alliances because they're interested in the overall portfolio.

Joining: Alliance Network Selection and Maintenance of Position in Alliance

If the Build or Join Tool pointed you to "joining," this section will set you on your way. You may not be able to configure an alliance portfolio around your firm, but if you have high attractiveness, you can still join an existing alliance network[2] and gain benefits from filling a valuable role in that network. By doing this you become a partner in another firm's portfolio and you will gradually become able to build your own. But, in the beginning, you don't control the portfolio, so you're really joining an alliance network, not building an alliance portfolio of your own. The central question is how to choose the alliance network to join. The answer turns out to be familiar. In Chapter 3, we discussed how important it is to consider the compatibility and complementarity of a potential alliance partner before joining an alliance, and the same principles apply when choosing an alliance network of another firm. A single alliance partner has a set of routines that are easy (or hard) to work with and may be trustworthy (or not). The same things apply for multiple partners in an alliance network which together bring information, cooperation, and power that can be complementary to yours, just as a single partner does.

Assessing compatibility and complementarity is not just a theoretical exercise. In the Introduction, we mentioned the research we've conducted on alliances in the shipping industry, where multiple firms join together in multi-party alliances to provide cost-effective transportation services for industrial customers who have high demands on frequency of departures, speed of delivery, and, above all, reliability. Shipping managers carefully assess potential partners for compatibility and complementarity before initiating an alliance. In this industry,

---

[2] Here, we refer to the alliance portfolio of another firm as an "alliance network."

compatibility can be measured by whether the ships are of comparable size and speed, but there are also intangible kinds of compatibility such as management style and reputation for quality and reliability. Managers also look carefully at complementarity, and they're especially interested in linking markets through alliances. Despite the careful checking shipping managers do before entering alliances, variation still exists in how high a level of compatibility and complementarity they achieve, and we found that firms that entered alliance networks with lower compatibility were less profitable.[3]

Joining an alliance network of another firm is like joining an alliance. There are two important things to do:

- **Look for a good fit.** You want to find a good fit between your firm and the other partners in the network, and a good fit means high compatibility and complementarity. The difference is that you look for compatibility and complementarity across the entire network, not just with your potential direct alliance partner or partners. Your firm will be most valuable as part of an alliance network to which it brings compatible and complementary capabilities, and it can keep its position in this network by maintaining the complementarity and using it to create value.
- **Check for network effectiveness.** Make sure the alliance network is effective. How well do its partners work together, and what results do they produce? Within an alliance network, your firm may start out with a single alliance, like a spoke in a hub-and-spoke portfolio, but if the network has an integrated structure overall, you can expect to have access to additional alliances with other firms in the network. In each

[3]Mitsuhashi, H. and H.R. Greve. 2009. A matching theory of alliance formation and organizational success: Complementarity and compatibility. *Academy of Management Journal* 52(5): 975–995.

alliance, you need to look once again for compatibility and complementarity as ways to contribute value.

When and How to Leave Alliances . . . And How to Plan for Termination

Alliances are formed to provide competitive advantage for the partners. Competitive advantage is not built overnight, so alliances typically succeed when they last for a while. That does not mean that they are supposed to be permanent. If you have joined an alliance network as a specialized or low-status player, then it is valuable to look out for other networks that have a greater potential for compatibility and complementarity. Changing is an option as long as it does not ruin your firm's network status. Industries differ in their norms for how long alliances typically last as well as in the contracts written to keep alliances together. If you're contemplating an alliance breakup, balance the opportunity for improving your position with the constraints given by the norms of your industry.

For example, our research on alliances in shipping showed that outside opportunities affected the stability of alliances. Firms compared their current alliance portfolio partners with firms outside the portfolio, and they were more likely to leave an alliance if they saw outside options with greater market complementarity.[4] These alliance portfolio changes make sense for shipping firms because their route networks get better when they have more complementary partners, and rapid changes of alliances are normal in shipping. As a result, alliances are often structured as short-term commitments that can be renewed if business conditions are favorable. That makes leaving an alliance easier, which fits shipping firms well because they often

---

[4] Greve, H.R., H. Mitsuhashi, and J.A.C. Baum. 2013. Greener pastures: Outside options and strategic alliance withdrawal. *Organization Science* 24(1): 79–98.

need to readjust their alliances to fit business conditions, and sometimes they use business conditions as an excuse to leave an alliance.

Similarly, if you have built an alliance portfolio of your own, there may be value in replacing partners with better ones. Again, impact on your network status needs to be a primary concern. By adding better partners with better resource complementarities or higher status, you can increase the network status of your firm and of the alliance portfolio in general.

It's also important to negotiate the process of exiting individual alliances and alliance portfolios at the time of joining them. Agreeing on trigger events is an important part of negotiating an alliance agreement. These are the events that will allow partners to end the alliance. Some of them include:

- alliance completion
- alliance performance failure
- collaborative deadlock.

Alliance completion defines the point at which you and your partners have reached the objectives you set out to achieve at the beginning of your collaboration. For example, in the pharmaceutical industry, a biotechnology firm and a big pharmaceutical firm might agree to terminate their alliance after the biotech firm has provided the pharmaceutical firm with enough drug targets to work on.

Alliance performance failure occurs when the alliance fails to reach the important milestones which were agreed upon at the beginning of the collaboration. These could be achieving minimum satisfaction levels for common customers, minimum volumes of joint sales by partners, minimum numbers of common customers served, or the like.

Collaborative deadlock involves execution of exit clauses stipulating termination of alliances if partners cannot agree on important decisions throughout the life of the alliance. The best cooperative agreements include dispute resolution mechanisms, including the formal process of escalating the deadlocked discussion to higher executive levels in the partner organizations, but if these fail, the partners need to agree that they are better off ceasing collaboration.

Another set of important issues involves ownership rights to the property used (or created) by the alliances. This property can include physical assets, such as buildings or permits, as well as intellectual assets such as patents, brands, or know-how. The higher the level of integration between the partners, the more difficult this separation becomes. However, it is still important to agree on the mechanism of the property split before you actually start collaborating. Discussing these issues with the partners early on can help you understand what they really want from the alliance, whether they're serious in committing to the relationship, and whether they will take a win–win approach to collaboration. If partners try to design most of the exit triggers to fit their requirements and are not willing to agree on fair distribution of the property ownership rights after termination, then it is likely to be a very difficult alliance for your firm and perhaps you need to look elsewhere for collaborators.[5]

While this sounds very legalistic, it's important to emphasize that initial discussion for the alliance termination events should not be done by the lawyers from both sides. Instead, the general framework for alliance termination (including trigger events and property separation) has to be agreed upon by the people who developed the business case for the collaboration and only then should the lawyers be involved. Discussing alliance

---

[5]This discussion on alliance exit draws heavily from Chapter 17 of Bamford, J., Gomes-Casseres, B., and Robinson, M. 2002. *Mastering Alliance Strategy: A Comprehensive Guide to Design, Management, and Organization.* Jossey-Bass. That chapter can be consulted for more in-depth treatment of exit clauses.

termination is a very sensitive matter and it's important to build trust between the business development teams from all sides before the lawyers start arguing about the details. If the lawyers fail to agree on something, then the business development people can intervene and influence their legal teams to find a compromise. However, if the lawyers are involved from the very beginning, the business development teams might not be able to generate enough trust between themselves, and this will prevent them from agreeing on anything.

Firms take different approaches to alliance termination. Razer, a computer and peripherals maker we discuss later in Chapter 10, prefers not to terminate its alliances. As long as a firm has the technological capabilities to supply a leading-edge technology in the future, it remains a partner even if Razer does not currently work with it on a specific development project or buy from it. Technological races in the computer industry are so rapid that leapfrogging is normal, so a company that misses in one technological generation may produce a hit in the next. Razer needs early and privileged access to information on new technologies, so it maintains partnerships. For the partners, this is also beneficial because Razer has a strong reputation for leading-edge products as well as high sales volumes of peripherals, so a partner would like to have its next generation technology adopted by Razer.

The shipping firm operates at the other end of the spectrum on alliance termination. It also assesses alliances based on goals. However, many of its alliances are time-limited agreements, so the decision facing the shipping manager is not whether to terminate an alliance, but whether to renew it. Shipping managers make sure that the alliance partner understands that the alliance will be assessed and by what criteria, and they clarify that there is nothing automatic in the continuation. This helps make alliance terminations a regular part of business rather than a potential source of conflict between the firms.

Going Forward

You've now seen how assessment of your firm's autonomy and attractiveness can help determine your strategy for making alliances. Having a strategy raises your game from being focused only on first-degree network advantages to pursuing the benefits of second- and third-degree network advantages. Now you have two choices: whether to build or join an alliance network and when and how to leave alliances. In the next chapter, you will see how firms develop patterns when they build their alliance portfolios. Recognizing these patterns will help you decide when and how you will benefit by changing your habits.

Chapter Highlights

- To achieve second- and third-degree network advantages, you need to choose between building your own alliance portfolio and joining the networks created by others.
- If your firm is high on attractiveness and autonomy, you should build alliance portfolios; if you're high on attractiveness but low on autonomy, you should join the networks built by others.
- If your firm is low on attractiveness but high on autonomy, you should invest in building your attractiveness by increasing your status, especially your track record as a great partner, and by creating your vision for an alliance portfolio. This will enable you to eventually build your own portfolio.
- If your firm is low on both attractiveness and autonomy, you need to invest in improving at least one of these dimensions.
- Assess the value of your alliance portfolio partnerships and leave alliances as needed while being mindful of the effect that the timing and the form of departure may have on your network status.

CHAPTER NINE

RECOGNIZING PATTERNS: TWO ALLIANCE PORTFOLIO-BUILDING STYLES

In 2008, when the global financial crisis and accompanying recession hit many manufacturing industries hard, Ford Motor Company took action to survive. Across the globe, major companies like Ford faced the prospect that they and their supply chains might unravel. Ford's managers realized they were threatened not only by their own cash problems but also by suppliers having cash-flow shortages if their customers (like General Motors or even Ford itself) cut back on spending. To allow Ford to retain its ability to manufacture cars and trucks at reasonable costs, its managers took bold steps to save their supplier relationships.[1] They started to systematically assess how much they needed each supplier, making plans to support the most important suppliers and contingencies to withdraw from the less important and weaker suppliers.

Ford managers thought they wouldn't be able to succeed on their own, so they contacted General Motors (GM) to

---

[1] The details of this case can be found in Hoffman, B.G. *American Icon: Alan Mulally and the Fight to Save Ford Motor Co.* Crown Business.

coordinate this effort. Why? GM and Ford shared many suppliers, and if Ford supported a supplier but GM halted orders, the supplier would still be likely to fail. Agreeing on which suppliers to retain would, in Ford's opinion, help rescue the manufacturing base for cars and trucks in North America. But GM refused to collaborate, citing possible antitrust violations. Ford managers doubted this was the real reason, but did not press GM further.

Instead, Ford reached out to its Japanese competitors and discovered that Toyota and Honda were extremely worried about losing their North American suppliers. When Ford told them that it had started to assess each supplier and make choices about which ones to support, they wanted to collaborate. As a result Ford, Toyota, and Honda made a joint effort to coordinate their supply decisions. This process sometimes involved "trading" suppliers because they didn't always agree on which ones they preferred to work with. Yet, the overall goal of preventing a collapse of the automobile parts supply chain in North America was so important that each automobile maker was willing to make some trades. They were also willing to engage in joint lobbying efforts to get U.S. government assistance. Again, GM did not participate. Ultimately Ford's efforts were successful because the three participating car makers were able to feed enough business to their critical suppliers. For both Ford and the Japanese automobile makers, maintaining local parts supply was (and is to this day) an essential element in their strategy for keeping manufacturing output flexible and inventory costs low.

Why did Toyota and Honda agree to work with Ford, while GM did not? The answer lies in their partnering patterns. We could have predicted this outcome because, just as people have habits that predict their future behaviors, a firm's past patterns of alliance portfolio-building activities foreshadow what it will do in the future. This telling proverb, often attributed to

Charles Reade, the nineteenth-century British novelist, describes this process:

> We sow a thought and reap an act; we sow an act and reap a habit; we sow a habit and reap a character; we sow a character and reap a destiny.[2]

Interestingly, firms also develop habits or, more precisely, patterns that help simplify decision making. These patterns can define their networks and their futures. Our research shows that firms develop strong patterns of behavior that are just as powerful as the individual habits that captured Reade's poetic attention.[3] When a firm forms relationships with a particular partner, it will continue forming relationships with this partner in the future. Similarly, once a firm learns how to build an alliance portfolio of a particular kind, it will continue in that pattern.[4] Such partnering patterns then form the firm's *alliance portfolio-building style*: its consistent pattern of alliance formation over time. This style emerges out of the two basic second-degree portfolio configurations that capture a firm's routine behaviors. Firms that start with hub-and-spoke portfolios develop a pattern of alliance formation where they continue to add more unconnected partners (spokes) to their portfolios and they don't encourage connections among the partners that

---

[2] http://en.wikipedia.org/wiki/Charles_Reade.

[3] Li, S.X. and T.J. Rowley. 2002. Inertia and evaluation mechanisms in interorganizational partner selection: Syndicate formation among U.S. investment banks. *Academy of Management Journal* 45(6): 1104–1120.

[4] Rowley, T., D. Behrens, and D. Krackhardt. 2000. Redundant governance structures: An analysis of structural and relational embeddedness in the steel and semiconductor industry. *Strategic Management Journal* 21: 369–386.

form the spokes of their portfolio. Likewise, firms that begin with integrated portfolios develop a pattern of continuing to incorporate new and interconnected partners into their portfolios and encouraging them to work together.

We start this chapter with a discussion of why patterns matter and how they can both help and hinder a firm's access to network advantage. Then, we present several examples showing how partnering patterns shape a firm's alliance portfolio-building style. You'll see that firms often have difficulty collaborating with other firms that have different styles. And, even when a firm realizes it must alter its portfolio-building style, change is difficult. We conclude with recommendations for how you can change your portfolio-building patterns and adjust your alliance portfolio-building style when needed.

If you can modify your alliance networking style, you're better able to gain second-degree advantages. Take Sony, for example, which we found to have the wrong alliance portfolio configuration when we applied the Configuration Alignment Tool (CAT) in Chapter 4. If a Sony manager agrees with this conclusion but can't adjust the firm's alliance portfolio-building style, the CAT won't be very helpful. Fortunately, it is possible to change—but difficult, we admit.

Why Patterns Matter

Alliances between firms can change more easily than the roads between towns in Roman Britannia, so one might think that alliance formation patterns can also change easily. Actually, it isn't. What if the Romans had been able to make direct connections between some of the towns that earlier had only been connected to Londinium? In principle that would have integrated the province better. But, in practice, the integration would have taken time. Merchant traffic was an important source of Londinium's prominence. Building a new direct road between two towns could have become a new trading route over time, but merchants with established trading partners would have found it easier and faster to continue using those established routes. Political power and status were also vested in the central city of Londinium, and would have been difficult for other towns to ignore. So even when the Romans created new roads in the network, use of the established routes did not change immediately.

Firms experience similar resistance to change because they establish patterns for how they handle alliances. These patterns give firms stability and reliability, ensuring that they fulfill the expectations of their alliance partners while producing network advantage for themselves. The patterns also form the foundation for learning how to improve within each alliance and transfer lessons from each alliance to subsequent alliances.

Patterns of building hub-and-spoke or integrated portfolios are important because they support internal capabilities and external predictability.

- **Patterns support internal capabilities.** Well-developed routines for finding potential partners make continuing the style more effective than changing to a different style. Managers who initiate alliances become committed to both the specific alliances they have created and the style of alliance portfolio these alliances form. This explains why one of the most difficult transitions a firm can go through is finding out that the alliance portfolio it started with is no longer appropriate for its current situation.
- **Patterns provide external predictability.** You and everyone around you can expect firms to stick to the styles they have adopted in the past. This means that if your firm considers an alliance with another firm, you will do well to discover the portfolio-building style of this prospective partner by investigating the structure of its alliance portfolio. This

information will be useful because it lets you know what type of portfolio you would enter if the alliance was established, and how you would be treated in this portfolio.

While patterns serve firms well in many instances, they can also reduce access to network advantage in other circumstances. Take, for example, firms with an integrated portfolio-building style. They work intensively to create benefits across alliances, and most of this work is done outside the firm. They have routines for initiating contact between alliance partners and helping them work together, but once these alliance partners have established a tie, the role of the firm at the center of the portfolio diminishes. As a result, compared to firms with a hub-and-spoke style, these firms that often leave much of the cross-alliance work to their partners are left with a reduced ability to learn across alliances.

If a firm with an integrated network style needs to integrate information in a hub-and-spoke fashion, it must acquire new patterns for collecting information from each alliance partner, integrating the information, and sending proposals to selected alliance partners regarding ways to profitably extract network advantage. These are patterns that firms with a hub-and-spoke style have honed for a long time, so making a transition from an integrated to a hub-and-spoke style implies an extended learning period before the firm can be fully effective.

Now, let's look at several cases that demonstrate how partnering patterns shape a firm's alliance portfolio-building style.

The Hub-and-Spoke Portfolio-Building Style: ARM and Apple

Advanced RISC Machines (ARM), an intellectual property supplier for semiconductor makers, designs semiconductor chips and has an especially strong market position in producing the reduced instruction set, low power consumption chips found in mobile phones and other devices that run on batteries. They don't make the chips they design. Instead, they license their designs to semiconductor manufacturers which make them and sell them to original equipment manufacturers (OEMs). In some cases, ARM licenses its designs directly to OEMs which then contract with semiconductor manufacturers to produce them or make them in their own plants.

The licensing agreements represent more than just a contract which allows the manufacturing of the semiconductor chips for a fee. ARM sees them as a "two-way" licensing model where the partners also provide information on how they use the chips.[5] Although partners are not allowed to modify the chip design in any way, they typically embed it in a shell of other chips and software to create a product that is unique, so mobile phones from different manufacturers are different from each other even though they all run on ARM chips. By learning enough about how this is done and what their partners plan in the future, ARM is able to design future chips that will also become industry standards because they meet the design requirements of all their customers, not just some.

This way of working with its alliance partners turns ARM into a broker of technology. It integrates the needs of its partners in order to create products that are valuable to all. The partners are competitors, so they would never want to be connected directly, nor would they accept any form of information leakage through ARM. But they accept and benefit from having ARM create products that meet the needs of all. By standardizing the basic processing functions of products such as the

---

[5]The model is described in "ARM Holdings Plc," INSEAD Case 302-170-1, by Eleanor O'Keefe and Peter Williamson. ARM has become much more dominant in its markets since the case was written.

processing chip used in mobile phones, ARM makes it cheaper for its alliance partners to develop the functions that differentiate their mobile phones from their competitors' phones. If ARM had been required to build such differentiation into the processing chip itself, it would have been much more expensive. By placing itself in the center of a network that contains all the major industry players, ARM also acquires third-degree advantages. It gains prominence as a chip supplier through its partners' prominence, and its reputation for quality grows because it has partners that care about quality components. Few other firms are connected to so many players in the mobile phone industry.

ARM serves as a good example of a firm that has developed a hub-and-spoke portfolio-building style. In each alliance, ARM looks for compatibility and complementarity to create value and realize first-degree advantage. But, it goes further by looking across alliances for brokerage opportunities that bring second-degree advantage. ARM draws knowledge from each alliance and actively looks for opportunities to use this knowledge to increase the value it provides in other alliances. When the alliances involve research and development, as in ARM's case, the brokerage involves integrating information gained from the different collaborations. ARM's alliance partners don't communicate directly because they compete with each other and don't want to reveal secrets. In essence, ARM has become a trusted broker and the only firm in the industry that partners can share development plans with.

Other firms that have a style of building hub-and-spoke portfolios may try to artificially keep their alliance partners separate. Apple, for example, is extremely secretive about the identity of its alliance partners and they are not allowed to provide information to the outside world showing that they work with Apple. This means that one partner working on a technology with Apple has no means of knowing that another partner is also working on the same technology with Apple. These partners can't connect, for example, to compare the terms on which they are working with Apple. Because there is so much value in being the "hub" firm that collects and integrates information, any direct connections between partner firms in a hub-and-spoke portfolio could eliminate the "hub" firm's brokerage role or make it less necessary. Then, firms like ARM and Apple would no longer be able to generate as much network advantage.

Patterns of Firms with Hub-and-Spoke Alliance Portfolio-Building Styles

As shown by the ARM and Apple examples, firms with a hub-and-spoke alliance portfolio-building style work intensively to generate benefits across alliances. However, the distinctive feature of such firms is that this work takes place within the firm, out of sight from its alliance partners. The firm's managers prefer to have first look at the potential results of their work and then present it to alliance partners in the form of proposals for finished products, new collaborative projects, and the like. The information behind these proposals is the "secret sauce" that the hub-and-spoke firm prefers to keep to itself. Its managers would rather not tell how they combined information across different alliance partners, and they would definitely be worried if these alliance partners started communicating directly. That could lead to them working together without the help of the broker firm acting as a necessary hub and prevent them from gaining the benefits associated with being the necessary hub. As a result of these patterns, the firm with a hub-and-spoke alliance portfolio-building style will have a strong bias against making cross-partner introductions.

They want to keep the second-degree advantages of being a hub to themselves.

The Integrated Portfolio-Building Style: Ford, Toyota, and Honda

Earlier in this chapter we explained Toyota's and Honda's cooperative actions by referring to their historic patterns. Both firms had always relied heavily on their suppliers, and have, in turn, been willing to support their most critical suppliers in times of trouble. They also had a tradition of distinguishing sharply between critical and non-critical suppliers—even to the point of being far less supportive of the non-critical suppliers. So it was natural for these carmakers to sort their suppliers by criticality during the 2008 crisis and focus on helping the critical ones. It's worth explaining how this pattern developed because it will help you understand how such patterns are born from specific situations and how sometimes situations change so much that the pattern no longer fits the company's needs.

If we go far enough back into the histories of Toyota and Honda, we can trace their reliance on suppliers to their birth and lengthy adolescence as cash-strapped firms. At this stage, they needed to focus on their core businesses and relied on suppliers out of necessity rather than choice. The U.S. automakers had a much more rapid path to success in a developed market and were able to integrate more of their parts manufacturing internally or place it for competitive bidding rather than form alliances. But among the U.S. automakers, the family-owned Ford Motor Company had closer relationships with its suppliers than GM did. GM was well known for pitting suppliers against each other in bidding wars. Although it had (and still has) alliances with other automakers, GM's usual way of handling suppliers was through market transactions rather than through alliances. In 2008 when the entire industry was thrown into a deep crisis and the context changed so much that it might have been wise to choose Ford's path of treating suppliers as a source of competitive advantage and even survival, GM did not change its patterns. In other words, Toyota and Honda were accustomed to helping their suppliers and building integrated portfolios with them. GM had a habit of pitting its suppliers against one another and building a hub-and-spoke portfolio that exploited suppliers' weaknesses. For the suppliers of Toyota, Honda, and Ford, this more cooperative pattern was certainly helpful in the crisis, and arguably it also helped Toyota, Honda, and Ford. In principle, though, there was no guarantee that an alliance portfolio-building style from 1950s Japan would fit a U.S. automaker in 2008.

Patterns of Firms with Integrated Alliance Portfolio-Building Styles

The firm with an integrated alliance portfolio-building style has a distinctive way of working with its partners. Like firms with a hub-and-spoke portfolio-building style, it looks for compatibility and complementarity in each alliance. And both firms get first-degree advantage in this way. However, the firm with the integrated portfolio style looks for compatibility and complementarity among its alliance partners, and it connects those that look like good matches and meet the overall objectives for its network portfolio. These connections are usually easy to understand from the viewpoint of the product or service architecture of the firm with an integrated portfolio configuration. The overall logic is to tie the alliance portfolio into a system in which any set of partners can respond autonomously to problems they face, without referring them to a central firm for resolution. This distributed problem solving is faster and more efficient than that of a hub-and-spoke portfolio firm, which is the reason the integrated portfolio coordinates complex tasks so well. Through this coordination, the firms in an integrated portfolio gain second-degree advantage.

Official histories of Toyota explain how its vaunted production system with close collaboration between Toyota and its parts manufacturers was designed to foster continuous improvements in design and manufacturing. In fact, the allocation of so much work to key parts manufacturers owed much to the economic constraints that Toyota had when it was established and sought to grow before World War II and in the post-war recovery period. The company lacked financing, technology, and markets for its cars, and it needed to conserve its resources as much as possible. Given these shortages, Toyota chose to build an integrated portfolio to conserve resources. For example, it let suppliers take over some engineering functions so that its in-house engineering department could focus on the most central functions of the car. However, to ensure that one supplier did not cheat Toyota or the other suppliers, it made sure that suppliers formed joint ventures (and made equity investments in each other), so that their individual success was strongly tied to the success of Toyota's integrated alliance portfolio. This approach proved successful, and was refined to become the process known as component design for manufacturing, which is one of the alliance activities that made Toyota and its alliance portfolio such potent competitors.[6]

Styles of Emerging Market and Developed Market Companies

Geographic origin often determines a firm's alliance portfolio-building style. In many emerging markets, alliances are used

---

[6]Fujimoto, T. 1999. *The Evolution of a Manufacturing System at Toyota*. Oxford University Press.

because the legal recourses for handling buyer–supplier exchanges that go wrong are weaker than in developed nations. Courts may be slow to decide, and damages paid for wrongdoing may be low or difficult to enforce. Under such conditions, forging an integrated portfolio of alliances may be a way to establish enough trust so that transactions can occur at all. There is research showing that firms in developing nations build alliance portfolios precisely for those parts of the business that involve valuable and uncertain exchanges. And, when an integrated alliance portfolio is put in place, firms let down their guard by using less complex contracts to govern the exchanges, and they experience increased performance. The increase in trust, achieved as a result of building an integrated portfolio, clearly works.

So, if the firm was started in an emerging market, it will be used to build integrated portfolios, which means that it will try to build closed ties with partners later in its life. If the firm was started in a developed market and especially in a highly competitive industry, it's likely to develop the style of building hub-and-spoke portfolios by forming open ties to partners. Later in its life, the firm will continue building hub-and-spoke portfolios, even if the environment changes or if it enters a developing market.

The use of alliances to substitute for legal mechanisms to enforce contracts in emerging markets represents a major difference from the role of alliances in developed markets. Overlooking this can be costly for a firm. A developed-market firm that enters an emerging market with the view that alliances are only needed when close coordination is called for might find itself handling late deliveries from suppliers and non-paying customers much more often than it anticipates. To reduce the number of problems it suffers from its partners, the firm entering the emerging market is advised to build closed ties with these partners. An emerging-market firm can also go wrong by overlooking how easily it can enter a developed market without building integrated portfolios.

How to Change Your Style

As you read the previous examples and explanations, did you recognize your firm? Are you able to see your alliance portfolio-building style? And do you think it might be beneficial for you to change in order to gain more network advantage?

As long as your preferred portfolio-building style matches the ideal portfolio you determined using the CAT, all is well. When there is a mismatch, however, you'll need to change your preferred style, which involves deliberately changing your patterns of alliance-building activities. Such a mismatch can result from changes in the factors summarized in the CAT. For example, your firm's environment may have become much more dynamic than before. If you prefer building an integrated portfolio, then you may have to learn how to build a hub-and-spoke one. Alternatively, if you are a highly diversified firm with a hub-and-spoke portfolio and you need to narrow the scope of your activities to specialize in a particular domain, you may have to learn how to build an integrated portfolio.

As we discussed earlier, the second driver for changing your firm's partnering style may be geographic expansion. Say your firm was founded in an emerging market, where the economic, legal, and social conditions are vastly different from those in the developed markets. If you want to enter a developed market now, you would have to change your alliance portfolio-building style. But, as with any organizational change, shifting from the hub-and-spoke style to integrated, or the other way around, can be very difficult. If you have ever tried to stop drinking coffee, you know that personal habits are hard to change. It's equally, if not more difficult for a company to change its patterns of behavior.

Table 9.1 Strategies to change your firm's partnering patterns

To build more open ties, you can form relationships with:	To build more closed ties, you can:
Makers of substitutes	Make referrals
Makers of complements	Neutralize a broker
New industry entrants	Seek referrals
Your partners' competitors	Form a union
Your direct competitors	

You can pursue several strategies to change your firm's partnering patterns and the corresponding portfolio-building style. In Chapter 5, we explored ways to identify new partners for building hub-and-spoke portfolios (adding more open ties) or integrated portfolios (adding more closed ties). These are summarized in Table 9.1.

How can these strategies be implemented so that you change your partnering patterns? To make the transition, you can try these three levers:

- Hire people with the right experience.
- Form ties for small wins.
- Partner with a firm that has the right patterns.

In the next few sections, we explain each of these strategies for changing your firm's partnering patterns and its corresponding alliance portfolio-building style.

Hire People with the Right Experience

To execute the activities needed to change your firm's alliance-building style, hire people who have experience with different portfolio-building strategies. For example, if you want to make your portfolio more hub-and-spoke, hire personnel who have experience in building and maintaining open ties. These people could come from competitors or partners that already have hub-and-spoke portfolios. In contrast, if you need to build a more integrated portfolio, hire alliance managers from companies that already have such portfolios. If you support them in bringing in new patterns and routines, these new hires can transplant the experience from their former place of employment.

Form Ties for Small Wins

Another way of changing your firm's partnering patterns is to proactively seek a closed or an open tie (depending on the style that has to be changed) and focus on achieving small wins in that relationship. That is, if you have a hub-and-spoke style and your portfolio needs to become more integrated, identify a group of potential partners that could reap some benefit from three-way collaboration and form a closed tie alliance with them to achieve some small success. Alternatively, if you have an integrated portfolio, build one open tie and learn how you can achieve small wins within this tie. Then, transfer information from this partner to your other partners. Learning from these successes, even though they are small, can help you understand how you can change your partnering patterns.

Partner with a Firm That Has the Right Patterns

If you want to change your partnering patterns, you can also form a tie with a partner that has the portfolio configuration you aspire to. By observing how this partner manages its alliance relationships, you can learn how to change your own partnering patterns. GM's 25-year partnership with Toyota in the NUMMI assembly plant provides a good example of this strategy. NUMMI was an old GM car assembly plant that was turned into a joint venture. GM and Toyota designed this alliance to jointly produce cars under their own brands as well as to facilitate learning from each other. Among other goals, Toyota wanted to learn how to build an alliance portfolio in the U.S. with the local suppliers that are accustomed to being spokes in the hubs of the automotive manufacturers' portfolios. GM wanted to learn how Toyota would structure its own relationships with the U.S. suppliers. What was most interesting, however, were the different approaches the two companies took to learning. GM sent its managers to observe what Toyota was doing; Toyota's managers actually participated in running the plant. As a result, GM was able to learn less about Toyota's approach to alliances, and Toyota was able to learn more about how to adapt its integrated portfolio approach to fit U.S. realities. The lesson: the best way to learn about how alliances work is to get involved with them and participate in their daily operations. Learning by observing is an inferior strategy to learning by doing.

Going Forward

Much of the discussion in this chapter (and in earlier chapters) implies that to benefit from your alliance portfolios, you need to be good at transferring information internally. This suggests the need for organizational structures and processes that help information flow freely between the people who manage individual alliances. This information flow helps firms realize the potential for first-degree network advantage and it especially promotes realizing second- and third-degree network advantage. In the next chapter, we examine what you can do internally to make sure you can reap the greatest network advantage now and in the future.

Chapter Highlights

- Firms develop patterns for how they approach alliance portfolio formation: a firm that started with a hub-and-spoke portfolio will find it easier to continue building such a portfolio, while a firm that started with an integrated portfolio will also find it easier to continue building an integrated portfolio.

- Changing the firm's portfolio configuration is a major operation because it means altering or replacing fundamental partnering patterns within the firm.
- Emerging market firms and developed market firms live in diverse environments. As a result, they develop different alliance portfolio-building styles and use alliances differently.
- Your firm can change its partnering patterns and portfolio-building style by:
  - hiring employees from companies that have the right partnering patterns
  - seeking small wins with a different kind of tie
  - partnering with a firm that has the right partnering patterns.

CHAPTER TEN

MANAGEMENT PRACTICES TO SUSTAIN NETWORK ADVANTAGE

What do food manufacturer Douwe Egberts/Sara Lee, beverage giant AB InBev, mobile phone maker Nokia, Internet communications company Skype, and Microsoft have in common? Each firm has partnered with Philips Electronics. In fact, during the period 2000 to 2011, Philips formed 91 alliances with partners in different industries. Philips epitomizes the kind of firm that generates innovations by seeing alliances as opportunities to blend and intertwine different types of businesses and industries. For example, Philips partnered with Douwe Egberts/Sara Lee to make Senseo coffee pod systems: Philips manufactured the coffee-making machine and Sara Lee roasted and packaged the coffee. The success of this partnership and the knowledge gained from it motivated Philips to form an alliance with AB InBev. This resulted in the creation of the Perfect Draft portable beer dispensing system composed of a dispensing device made by Philips and a beer keg made by AB InBev. Philips also provides an excellent example of a firm adept at absorbing the information and knowledge flowing across its alliance network and spreading it to other parts of the organization. This concept of transferring models and learning is at the heart of realizing the fullest form of network advantage across an enterprise and sustaining it over the long term.

Up to now we've discussed where network advantage comes from and how different alliance portfolios lead to different degrees of advantage. We've described the *potential* of your network. However, you won't automatically realize that potential. To make it happen and sustain it over time, you need to have an internal organization and rigorous processes that help your firm look *across* alliances for opportunities. These elements promote internal coordination to ensure new knowledge, gained from healthy information exchanges with partnerships, flows to others in the organization and is used to improve existing businesses or create new ones. Samsung was able to develop and transfer knowledge across its partnerships better than Sony, and as a result Samsung became more innovative while Sony lost its technological edge and its cool image. It's clear from Samsung's advertising and product announcements that the firm has lost interest in competing with Sony and is instead gunning for Apple. Witness its 2012 ads depicting iPhones as less capable than its own phones or its 2013 launch of a mobile phone with movement-tracking features that far exceed the capabilities of iPhones. As discussed in Chapter 2, this was not just a result of the different alliance portfolios that Samsung and Sony created. Samsung also employed a set of management practices designed to realize its network advantages. In this chapter, let's look at the management practices used by firms that successfully generate first-, second-, and third-degree network advantages and why these practices work. To learn about these management practices, we interviewed executives at companies that faced and overcame the challenge of managing information flows to achieve network advantage. We share their real-life advice to guide you through similar challenges.

Managing Information Flows

The first challenge in realizing network advantages is to make sure your company communicates internally. Even though we depict organizations in our network pictures as single circles, firms like Philips, Intel, Samsung, Sony and the other companies discussed in this book are not monolithic entities. Each of these organizations has multiple units that may manage products, markets or regions. And each of these units is also a circle, so these organizations are best seen as a cluster of circles that may or may not share the insights and knowledge gained from their partnerships. Most of the time, alliances are "owned" by the individual units of the organizations whose main job is to produce first-degree network advantage from the alliances. Yet, network advantage on the enterprise level comes from having these units aggregate knowledge for the purpose of gaining second- and third-degree network advantages. To achieve this objective, for example, the manager in charge of Philips's alliance with AB InBev needs to be able to talk to the manager in charge of the Senseo alliance as well as the managers responsible for alliances with Swarovski Crystal, Nokia and Microsoft.

If you work in a large company, you know that we are describing a challenge common to many functions. Alliance management is no different: you will have to overcome your company's size to realize your network advantage. If the partnerships that have the potential to create your second-degree network advantage exist in different parts of the company, then, unless properly managed, that network advantage will remain unrealized. If you have a hub-and-spoke portfolio, it's especially likely that these partnerships are separated from each other because the spokes often go to partners that are very different from each other, and they involve different activities. But even integrated portfolios will fail to produce network advantages if your company is not integrated internally.

Small companies like Floating Power Plant (see Chapter 7) often have less difficulty sharing knowledge and managing information flows than giants such as Philips and Samsung, because the decision making is confined to a small group of people who know all about their alliances and can think about creating value across them. Some of the practices we describe in this chapter do not fit small companies. However, it's useful to consider knowledge sharing as early as possible so that the advantage of smallness does not disappear. As companies grow in size expanding to multiple businesses, divisions, and/or geographies, knowledge transfer becomes problematic. When we talked with Iain Ross, the Group Managing Director at WorleyParsons, a large Australian provider of project delivery and consulting services for the resource and energy sectors, he captured the essence of this problem: "Once you are creating and actually relying on job descriptions to organize your company, knowledge does not automatically flow . . . it has to be managed."

Alliance Management Offices

At Philips, John Bell accepted the challenge of sharing knowledge across divisions. He started the Alliance Office in 2000, and in 2013 was appointed Head of Strategy and Partnerships at Philips Research. Even though the Alliance Office has always had fewer than a handful of employees, its role is vitally important for Philips's future because it coordinates the company's alliance activities in a way that aims to realize second- and third-degree network advantages. Practices centralized in this office help knowledge cross business units.

Alliance management offices have different names in different organizations. Some common ones are "The Office of Alliance Management," "Business Development Team," or even "Innovation and Market Access Department." Despite the big names, these offices tend to be small. In most companies we interviewed, they are staffed by a maximum of a dozen executives, and there are between four and eight executives responsible for this centralized alliance management function. The big names serve a purpose: they underline the central role of these offices in building the network advantage. Adding to that signal, alliance management offices get a position in the formal organizational hierarchy that signals their strategic importance. In most companies with a successful alliance management system, this office reports directly to the senior leadership team. This ensures senior leadership involvement in alliance management.

Failing to involve senior executives in managing alliances typically leads to under-investment in them. For example, when we interviewed a European executive in a global automotive parts supplier, we found that although this company has a significant share in the automotive parts market, it has a dismal track record in building and managing alliances. Its only successful alliance is with a Japanese partner and it works because top executives from the global headquarters of both companies are involved. These executives hold regular meetings where they discuss the progress of the alliance and make sure it has the resources it needs to continue operating. The European executive realized that the firm's other alliances failed to deliver because they did not get the attention of top management at global headquarters. Interestingly, this alliance is handled differently precisely because the Japanese firm demands top executive involvement of its partners in order to ensure alliance success.

In many cases, executives responsible for alliance management also work closely with the business development executives responsible for mergers and acquisitions (M&As). This should not be a surprise because alliances and M&As represent different answers to the same problem. When an organization doesn't have a particular resource or capability, it must decide whether to build it internally, buy it through an acquisition, or borrow it through alliances. The strategic decision to build, buy or borrow depends on the attractiveness of each option.[1] Philips has an M&A department which works closely with the alliance management office to determine the relative merits of these options.

Alliance Management DNA

Not all managers in the companies we interviewed believed it was necessary to create an alliance management office. But the firms that did not centralize the function of knowledge sharing across alliances and were still successful in realizing their network advantage were alliance-obsessed in other ways. They relied so heavily on alliances to implement their business strategies that all managers knew the importance of probing for alliance knowledge and opportunities. Internally, they were trained in alliance management practices and kept each other updated on what alliances they were working on; externally, they were looking for promising alliance partners. You could say that these companies had managed to embed alliance management practices into their DNA. These firms were the exceptions to the rule: there was little need to centralize or motivate knowledge sharing across alliances because managers

---

[1] Our colleagues Laurence Capron and Will Mitchell wrote an excellent book, *Build, Borrow or Buy: Solving the Growth Dilemma* (2012, Harvard Business Review Press), where they examine conditions under which firms should develop resources and capabilities internally or look for them outside through alliances or acquisitions.

in different divisions and geographies themselves sought out colleagues involved in different partnerships. Knowledge sharing happened naturally.

Indeed, for a large Internet firm we interviewed, an alliance management office would become a bottleneck in its operations because there are simply too many alliances for a single office to handle. For convenience, alliance management in this firm is organized geographically, but alliance managers are expected to reach out across geographies when necessary. They have a knowledge management system to help them find peers with the right expertise and partnership portfolio, but mainly the alliance managers rely on their own skill and personal networks inside the firm. It's their job to know who to contact for particular expertise. Managers in firms like this look for alliances the way bees look for nectar in flowers. They spread out to find opportunities one by one, and they return to tell the others what they have found and get help if they need it.

Management Practices Needed to Realize First-Degree Advantage

Whether or not the task of alliance management is centralized in a dedicated department, the objective is clear. It's critical to manage information and knowledge flow in order to realize your firm's potential network advantage. First, it's necessary to ensure that the benefits of each individual partnership can be obtained. As discussed in Chapter 1, the formation of a partnership does not guarantee the flow of required resources and knowledge into an organization. Alliances can be delicate, requiring relationship-building skills that promote trust, mutual gain and a long-term orientation. These skills are important because only healthy partnerships generate knowledge flow. And, quite frankly, without experience, many managers lack these skills. So, managers often need help with recognizing partners with the best fit and building trust in the partnership.

The Alliance Office at Philips helps business unit executives across the organization select alliance partners, negotiate terms of collaboration, evaluate alliance progress, and unwind alliances that have run their course. This support ensures that the benefits sought from each partner flow into the organization. Whether through an alliance management office or through having alliance management DNA embedded in the organization, every firm needs to establish a set of management practices designed to realize first-degree network advantages.

Partner Selection

Many companies get offers to initiate partnerships; sometimes they get lots of offers. These may include some diamonds in the rough, but typically alliance portfolios generate greater returns if the company has a set of practices for finding good alliance partners. Forming alliances involves a matching process, and in matching processes the party that takes the initiative does best. Partner selection practices are founded on industry expertise, but they go beyond expertise on what characterizes the industry to include processes for using it for forming valuable alliances. Because first-degree advantage is known and exploited by many firms already, these practices usually include some way of making sure that an alliance management office or the unit managers use evaluation models like the Four Dimensions of Fit we discussed in Chapter 3. Philips uses a proprietary model similar to the First-Degree Assessment Tool. It does this assessment by involving both unit managers and the Alliance Office. For example, an executive from the Lighting Sector who proposes a particular alliance has to work closely with the Alliance Office and other senior executives to ensure that the proposed alliance is more attractive than other possible alliances or accomplishing the task internally.

It's also common practice to collect information about potential partners and make sure it's easy for unit managers to access this information when they're looking for alliance partners. The way this is done varies greatly. We talked to an alliance officer who pointed to his head when we asked him where the company's information about potential partners is stored. In high-tech industries, firms use the technology office as a store of information on potential partners. The large Internet firm we interviewed had a computerized knowledge management system. If the company has one, the alliance management office is the most natural place to store information about potential partners.

If no central repository exists, unit managers are often trained to search systematically using the external information that is most important for their businesses. The large Internet firm relies on each manager having local expertise, and it uses formalized criteria to search for alliance partners. One manager we spoke to referred to those criteria as the "tangibles," and noted that they were needed in order to start a conversation to reveal the "intangibles" of how the firms worked that would help them determine whether the firms fit together. A shipping firm we interviewed used the same process. It searched for information on strategic and resource fit using tangibles such as the market areas served and the ships used. These were simple to find using industry reference books, so the firm could easily assess many potential alliance partners. The Internet firm and shipping firm businesses have nothing in common, but they share a reliance on alliances and a proactive process for selecting partners.

Alliance Initiation

Alliance initiation is also governed by a set of practices that are either shared across alliance managers in each unit or enforced by the alliance management office. Companies that have many alliances typically do this in a very routine fashion, and the routine includes assessment points which allow them to stop the process if they discover misfits that were not apparent in the partner selection stage. Success in the alliance initiation stage is not necessarily defined by forming an alliance; it can also be achieved by avoiding an alliance that would have been difficult to manage. The shipping firm we interviewed was clear on the need to assess fit through the alliance initiation stage. Once it found a promising partner, it started conversations and relied on reputation to determine the culture fit. We interviewed a high-tech firm that was less concerned with culture fit because its overriding goal was having the best technology available at all times. As a result, it was mainly interested in whether the technology offered by a potential partner was a good fit for its products. To validate that, this firm moves to actual testing of the technology as soon as possible, and it lets the evaluations made by the design teams determine whether to go ahead with a specific technology or not.

Alliance Problem Solving

Firms are strong alliance partners when they provide a single point of contact to make problem solving in the alliances easy for the partners. There is nothing more frustrating for a partner than not knowing who to contact when it has a problem. The best alliance managers intimately understand the partner's problems and are able to solve them as effectively as possible. In some of the firms we interviewed, the alliance manager was empowered to do this independently, so the partner would rarely deal with others in the organization except in a supporting role. In other firms, the alliance manager has the authority to refer the partner to the appropriate manager in their own company, even if this manager is not the "owner" of the alliance from the functional unit.

This structure with a single point of contact is not just a way to solve problems. It also clarifies who the partner can talk to if they want to expand the alliance to cover new activities. An important part of first-degree advantage is how well partners work over time to make the relationships more valuable. Typically, you will treat a new partner with caution because you don't know how capable and reliable that partner is. Caution protects against the downside, but it also limits the upside of value generated in a relationship. Once the partner firm has proven its worth, either you or the partner may be interested in expanding the relationship to add more value. If this is a complicated process that involves the same steps as making a new alliance, it's hard to do. If the process can be done by working through the current alliance manager, the relationship grows naturally. This involves giving your alliance manager enough power to guide the firm through a change in the relationship, often working directly with higher management levels or the alliance management office.

A very important set of alliance management tasks focuses on managing change. Alliance partners may have goals and capabilities that change over time; they may change their assessments of each other as they build mutual trust or the markets may change. It's unrealistic to enter an alliance with the assumption that it will never need to be changed. This process is straightforward as long as the changes are intended to accomplish the original goals of the alliance and add new goals, but not all change occurs through simple addition. Alliances may improve, at least in the eyes of one partner, if some activities are replaced by others, for example. This is difficult because the partners may see different costs and benefits associated with the change. Sometimes partners disagree on whether an alliance needs to change and how, so a strong process for making changes has to be in place. What's most important is ensuring that the process handles changes in the scope of the alliance without hurting the firm's reputation as a good alliance partner. This will only happen if the process is fair and transparent. Typically, that means linking it closely to a formal alliance assessment process.

Alliance Assessment

Over the life of an alliance, alliance managers at Philips and executives from the business unit that "owns" the alliance periodically review its progress. To make sure this evaluation is done with information from both their own organization and the partner, executives from both partner companies respond to a survey in which they rate the alliance using criteria similar to the Four Dimensions of Fit that we discussed in Chapter 3. Because Philips's business unit managers and managers from the partner complete the survey independently, they can compare answers and understand how the alliance might be seen differently from each side. During this comparison, managers from the Alliance Office are present to facilitate the discussion. The goal is to judge the overall health of the alliance and produce ideas on how to improve it.

The large Internet firm we interviewed doesn't have an alliance management office. Instead, this firm lets each unit's alliance manager evaluate alliances. To ensure this is done in a uniform way across alliances along with alliance partner managers, the firm adopts a formalized approach. For each alliance, the alliance manager and the partner set key performance indicators (KPIs) during the alliance negotiations. These are objectives they agree are necessary in order to declare the alliance successful and to continue investing the resources allocated to it. After that, both parties follow the KPIs very frequently, and they also stay in touch to find out the story behind the KPIs. They call each other and send email messages so that each partner knows what the other is thinking about the alliance and what it is doing to improve its results. They want to make sure that there's constant comparison between what the alliance yields and what the partners signed up for. This way, there's no argument over whether to continue an alliance as before or change the resources allocated to it. The partners can tell in real time if it delivers or not, and if it fails to deliver they will scale it down by mutual agreement. It's unusual for this firm to terminate alliances; instead it reduces the resources invested in an alliance if it does not produce the intended results.

Management Practices Needed to Realize Second- and Third-Degree Advantages

The alliance practices we've discussed so far help to realize first-degree advantage, but they are only the first step toward realizing your network advantage. Next comes the hard part. In addition to enhancing the flow of knowledge from the network of partnerships into the organization, you need to make knowledge flow across the organization rather than leaving it in the pool where it entered. Easier said than done, we know. Information sharing across units is rather uncommon given unit-level business differences, distance, and sometimes internal politics or competitiveness. Philips has multiple offices located around the world to help information gained from alliances flow across markets and geographies. Despite being scattered across thousands of kilometers and focused on its own objectives and budgets, Philips recognizes that business units possess knowledge useful to others. Its Alliance Office seeks to facilitate the internal knowledge flow between these business units.

Consider Philips's strategy in the home coffee-brewing market mentioned earlier in this chapter. The collaboration between Philips and Sara Lee began in 2001. The partners made the Senseo coffee system which was capable of making one or two cups of coffee and was designed to capitalize on the growing luxury market for espresso and cappuccino. This product represented one way to generate new revenue in a stabilizing coffee market. Philips made the machine into which one poured water and inserted a concentrated coffee capsule. Sara Lee supplied the coffee capsules. Senseo was hugely successful and in just four years it reached 10 million customers. Putting together this product required Philips to understand how to integrate and sell complementary products (machines and capsules) as well as how to divide this value given that they had to sell one part of the offering—the coffee-making machine—at a discount and recuperate the lost revenues by selling the capsules. The process of deciding what value is contributed by each party and how to divide the value generated from the partnership has crippled many alliances before they even got started.

The Senseo success story is extraordinary because Sara Lee and Philips overcame this challenge. It would have been easy to develop and apply this knowledge once and then declare victory. Instead, the Alliance Office saw this alliance as a template and looked for ways to use it again. It applied these lessons to the creation of PerfectDraft, which used the same concept: Philips made the beer dispenser while AB InBev made the beer. In both cases, the Alliance Office facilitated the internal discussions that led to the recognition and development of the opportunity.

Building an Internal Network

Firms that successfully build and sustain network advantage talk internally about alliances—a lot. Whether an alliance management office exists or not, alliance managers know that they are not alone, and they can improve the alliances they manage and find opportunities for new ones by working together with other alliance managers. Essentially, they form an informal network inside their firm that manages its alliance network of the firm.

This internal network helps share information about individual alliances so that others can build knowledge about the alliance portfolio and generate better ideas. This is not always easy. For example, we interviewed executives in a large U.S. financial services firm that has a significant insurance business. In the U.S., its alliance portfolio is configured as a hub-and-spoke. The firm creates retail financial products, such as insurance policies, annuities and mutual funds, and sells them through hundreds of spokes, which are the firm's distributors: banks, brokerage firms and insurance agents. One key alliance opportunity for the firm is to connect itself to partners in Europe and Asia that also have "spokes" of their own. The idea is to build a multi-hub model where the firm becomes a global "hub of hubs." These additional hubs would then distribute the firm's products worldwide.

This firm does not have a centralized alliance management function. Most of its alliances happen opportunistically, but there are many top executives who feel the need to create this kind of function so that learning about partnerships flows across business units. As one executive put it, "there are trillions of dollars' worth of opportunities in the U.S. and around the world, and we can realize these opportunities through alliances." In order to capitalize on more of these opportunities, the firm's senior executives in charge of different geographical business units now meet regularly to discuss what's going on in different parts of their organization. These face-to-face meetings build good working relationships between the senior executives and help them to enable information flows across the organization and identify business opportunities across alliances.

Helping Partners Build Their Networks

When we interviewed the large Internet company, they told us they use a business model that starts by forming partnerships with firms that have complementary businesses. But, the next step is equally important: they work to help the partners develop their businesses through new services. They do this either within a hub-and-spoke portfolio in which they continue to work exclusively with the partner or by connecting the partner to other complementary partners in the firm's portfolio. As an alliance manager explained, "We need to connect everyone and help everyone. In our kind of business it doesn't pay to look too carefully at what portion you get because as long as you're at the fulcrum you'll get a piece of the business. The main part is to grow the pie, because then our business also grows."

Configuring relationships between partners is also a key role for Lee-Yang Lau, senior business development officer of Razer, which makes high-end personal computers and peripherals, and has a broad range of partnerships. Some are long-lasting and very successful partnerships such as the alliance with chip maker NXP (formerly a Philips unit) for supplying high-end sensor chips to Razer for its computer mice. Others are activated depending on which firm has the best technology at the time. Razer has a technology office that keeps track of the technological developments of partner firms, including potential partners that approach them with new technologies. The technology office and the design teams work together when a promising technology becomes available and needs to be tested, and they proactively ask partners with complementary capabilities to work with each other in order to benefit (or just test) this technology.

Thinking across Alliances: The Jigsaw Tool

These management best practices are important for realizing the network advantage. But they don't automatically help companies realize second-degree advantage by combining resources and lessons *across* partners. Executives in companies like Philips, Razer and the Floating Power Plant intuitively think across alliances. Here's an example showing how this works. Lavazza, an Italian coffee-maker, started a partnership with Handpresso, a firm that had developed innovative technology for a hand-held machine with a manual pump that generated enough pressure to make high-quality espresso. They signed an exclusive partnership to develop and market a machine that fit Lavazza's coffee capsules. Handpresso signed the contract with Lavazza because Lavazza had a connection to Fiat and Handpresso had already designed an espresso machine for the car. Soon afterward, Lavazza introduced Handpresso to Fiat, which was interested in an accessory customers could use to make espresso in their cars. This led to a partnership in which Handpresso developed a machine that used the power outlet of the new Fiat 500 and was marketed as an accessory to it. Naturally, the machine used Lavazza coffee capsules and this featured prominently in the marketing of this car in Italy.

Similarly, Singapore's Agency for Science, Technology and Research presented Razer with a carbon fiber solution for plastics. Razer was interested but not sure whether it could be manufactured at the scale needed, so it made an introduction to one of its alliance partners and left the collaboration to proceed on its own. With minor tweaks to the raw material and the manufacturing process, the new carbon fiber solution was transformed from a low-volume, lab-produced product to a high-volume, mass-producible product.

Ideas like these seem very natural once they exist, but developing them isn't as easy as it seems. To assist you in discovering alliance opportunities and making decisions about which ones to pursue, we created the final tool in the Toolbox— the Alliance Portfolio Jigsaw. Figure 10.1 summarizes the steps involved with using this tool.

Figure 10.2 shows an example of what a completed Alliance Portfolio Jigsaw might look like for a fictional firm, Omega Production, and its three partners which we call Alpha Research

Figure 10.1: Steps in the Alliance Portfolio Jigsaw Tool

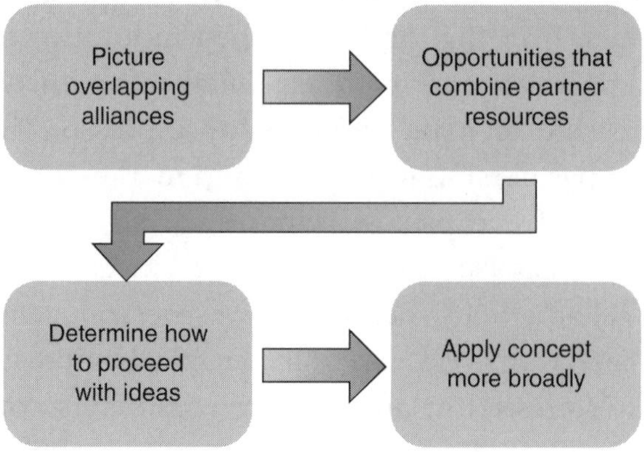

Institute, Beta Hospital and Gamma Software, shown in a portfolio configuration inspired by Philips's experiences.

Step 1: Picture Overlapping Alliances

The first step of this exercise is to pick three or four key alliance partners that your firm has now. For each partner, identify your firm's current objective for working with this partner and the resources each partner currently has. Keep the category of partner resources intentionally broad and include intangible resources, tangible resources and social resources (in other words the partner's ties to others).

In Figure 10.2, you can see that Omega Production is doing joint research with Alpha Research on creating new LED technologies. Omega supplies medical equipment to Beta Hospital. Omega also bundles its hardware together with Gamma's software and sells its product to different customers.

Step 2: Conceptualize Opportunities That Combine Partner Resources

Now take each pair of partners (the overlapping circles) and think about projects or initiatives your firm can start if you combine the resources from each one of them.

Figure 10.2: Sample Alliance Portfolio Jigsaw Tool

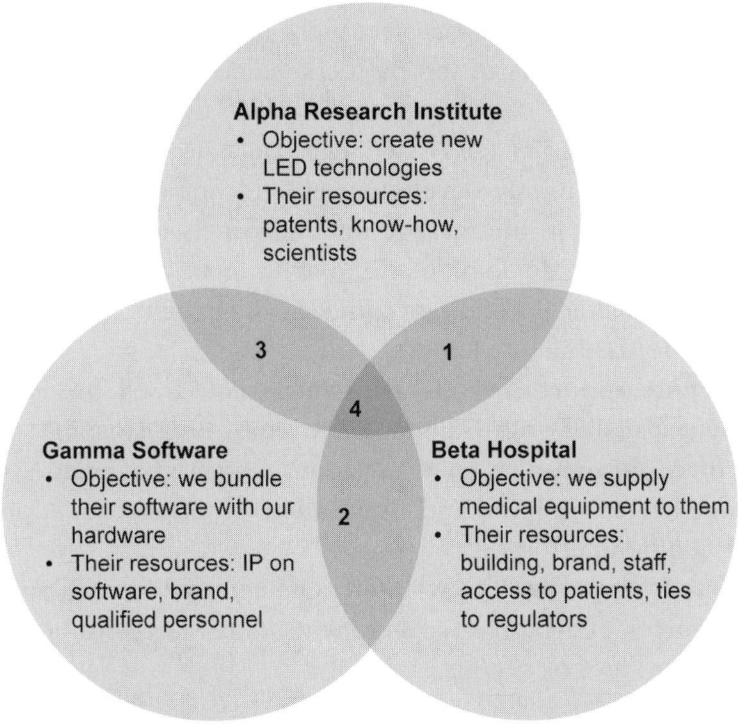

Alpha Research Institute
- Objective: create new LED technologies
- Their resources: patents, know-how, scientists

3   1

4

Gamma Software
- Objective: we bundle their software with our hardware
- Their resources: IP on software, brand, qualified personnel

2

Beta Hospital
- Objective: we supply medical equipment to them
- Their resources: building, brand, staff, access to patients, ties to regulators

1 Do research and make light panels to facilitate recovery of patients, and improve the well-being of hospital personnel

2 Sell hospitals our equipment run by our partner's software (e.g. we sell hardware to do medical tests, partner sells data aggregation software)

3 Provide a research institute with our equipment and partner's software on data aggregation to increase the speed of data analysis

4 A three-way partnership

Figure 10.2 shows four possible opportunities that could be generated by Omega Production using the Alliance Portfolio Jigsaw. We refer to Omega's partners in each opportunity by using the first letters of the partners' names.

- **First opportunity (A+B):** Omega could use the knowledge gained from jointly developing LED technology with Alpha and integrate it into making lighting panels for sale to Beta. It could also do joint research with Beta to examine the specific medical conditions under which light therapy can provide the highest impact.
- **Second opportunity (G+B):** Omega could sell the equipment it makes with Gamma Software to Beta Hospital.
- **Third opportunity (A+G):** Gamma and Alpha could work together to find ways to use Gamma's software in Alpha's data-mining efforts.
- **Fourth opportunity (A+B+G):** Omega could combine the resources of all three partners with its resources to create a new product or service.

You can repeat this exercise with different partner configurations in order to identify opportunities for greater network advantage in each configuration.

Step 3: Determine How to Proceed with Ideas

Next, decide whether you want to realize these opportunities as part of a hub-and-spoke or an integrated portfolio. This decision depends on your firm's optimal portfolio configuration as indicated by your CAT (see Chapter 4). Looking at Figure 10.2, if Omega Production is in a stable industry, has low market power or is a specialist, then it's probably better off bringing two of its partners together for initiatives A+B, G+B, or A+G—that is, if they can collectively agree on an integrated three-way collaboration. If Omega Production is in a more dynamic industry, has higher market power or has a broad product range, it could try to keep these partners separate and realize the network advantage by continuing to play a hub role between them.

Step 4: Apply the Concept More Broadly

You can do this same exercise with the list of potential partners you generate using the Second-Degree Assessment Tool (see Chapter 5). That is, you can pick some makers of complementary products, makers of substitutes, new industry entrants, or your competitors and ask yourself whether you could create new and valuable combinations by collaborating with them as well as with your existing partners. This means adding more circles to your Jigsaw and then indicating in each circle what resources you could get from these potential partners and thinking through new combinations that you could create with them.

You can also use this tool to think about opportunities for realizing third-degree network advantages. That is, which firms among the potential partners you identified above have high status? The high-status partner identification exercise in Chapter 7 gives you a place to start. By identifying opportunities for collaboration between your current partners and the high-status partners you don't have a tie with yet, you'll not only create something new but also enhance your own status. And, if you see valuable combinations that could be created between your existing partners and a potential high-status partner, make sure the high-status partner knows about these valuable resource combinations. This can be done without revealing which of your partners are the sources of these resources, at least initially. By generating such combinations of resources, you can show the high-status partner the value of collaborating with you.

We recommend that you organize portfolio evaluation sessions using this tool at least every six months and involve the line executives who are in charge of different alliances. Of course, the people chosen to work on this idea generation will vary depending on the available expertise in each business. These sessions are not effective if only alliance managers attend because the executives in the business units that are operationally involved with the alliances have the necessary knowledge about the technological, product, and market opportunities.

Going Forward

If you're thinking that unlocking your network advantage is hard work, you're right. That's why its benefits come to those companies that not only commit to pursuing this aspect of competitive advantage but also integrate that pursuit into their structures, systems and culture. The most successful firms have top executives, alliance managers and functional unit executives who work together to build and sustain this potent source of competitive advantage. In this last sentence, it's the key words "work together" that make all the difference. In our experience, second- or third-degree network advantage is rarely realized by one person alone. You will achieve much better results when you integrate the ideas and networks of your colleagues into your approach.

We invite you to use the templates in the Toolbox to involve your colleagues in strategic evaluation, thinking and planning for your network advantage strategy. Think of yourself as a Roman senator in charge of the collaboration required to build roads to cities. Will the highway network that you build take your firm to sustained and profitable growth? We certainly hope so and wish you "bona fortuna"—"good luck" in Latin—as you identify and leverage information, cooperation and power for your network advantage.

Chapter Highlights

- Firms need to implement a set of management practices to realize and sustain first-, second-, and third-degree network advantages.
- The companies that realize network advantage do so with the help of either:
    - an alliance management office that has strong top management support; or
    - an alliance-focused strategy that facilitates internal knowledge sharing without an alliance management office.
- The management practices that help firms realize first-degree network advantage involve knowledge sharing within the organization to aid in:
    - partner selection
    - alliance initiation
    - alliance problem solving
    - alliance assessment.
- The management practices that help firms realize second- and third-degree network advantage call for building informal networks within the organization to share knowledge about how each partner can create value when working with you and your other partners.
- The Alliance Portfolio Jigsaw Tool helps you identify business opportunities across your alliances in a systematic fashion.

ABOUT OUR RESEARCH

Academic Background

This book is an outcome of close to 40 years of collective academic research on alliances. Together, we have published about 30 studies on alliances in leading academic peer-reviewed journals. We have interviewed many executives and taught hundreds of executive program participants at INSEAD (France/ Singapore/Abu Dhabi/Moscow) and the University of Toronto between 2000 and 2012.

Table A.1 summarizes selected studies that were published in the academic journals. These studies guided us in creating the frameworks in this book.

In addition to our own research cited in Table A.1, our frameworks also tremendously benefited from studies by other researchers. These are identified in the footnotes in each chapter.

Mapping the Networks

This section will explain the process of creating alliance portfolio maps used in the book. Business executives interested in visualizing networks of their firms and thinking through the steps needed to extract network advantage should refer to

Table A.1 Selected studies

Cited in:	Full reference	Sample	Key insights
Introduction, Chapter 3	Mitsuhashi, H. and H.R. Greve. 2009. A matching theory of alliance formation and organizational success: Complementarity and compatibility. *Academy of Management Journal* 52(5): 975–995	Data on shipping line operators originating from 37 nations. The data extend from 1988 through 2005	Firms look for compatibilities and complementarities when forming alliances
Chapter 1	Greve, H.R. 2009. Bigger and safer: The diffusion of competitive advantage. *Strategic Management Journal* 30(1): 1–23	Data on liner and oil tanker shipping firms adopting innovations	Information advantages from networks help firms adopt innovations that give competitive advantage
Chapter 1	Bowers, A., H.R. Greve, H. Mitsuhashi, and J.A.C. Baum. Forthcoming. Competitive parity, status disparity, and mutual forbearance: Securities analysts' competition for investor attention. *Academy of Management Journal*	Data on security analyst estimates from 1995 to 2007	Information and cooperation advantages from networks give competitive advantage

Chapter 3, Chapter 5	*Louis Vuitton Moët Hennessy (LVMH): The rise of talentism.* INSEAD case studies written by Nancy Leung under supervision of Frederic Godart and Andrew Shipilov	Over 20 interviews with top executives in LVMH which were conducted in 2012	Practical usefulness of the Four Dimensions of Fit framework / Mapping second-degree networks
Chapter 4	Rowley, T., D. Behrens, and D. Krackhardt. 2000. Redundant governance structures: An analysis of structural and relational embeddedness in the steel and semiconductor industries. *Strategic Management Journal* 21: 369–386	Data on global semiconductor and steel-making companies between 1990 and 1996	Firms in highly uncertain industries need to build hub-and-spoke networks, while firms in more stable industries need to build integrated networks
Chapter 4	Shipilov, A.V. 2006. Network strategies and performance of Canadian investment banks. *Academy of Management Journal* 49(3): 590–604	Investment banks participating in the market for new securities in Canada between 1952 and 1990	Diversified firms benefit from hub-and-spoke networks more than all other firms

(Continued)

Table A.1 (*Continued*)

Cited in:	Full reference	Sample	Key insights
Chapter 4	Shipilov, A.V. 2009. Firm scope experience, historic multimarket contact with partners, centrality, and the relationship between structural holes and performance. *Organization Science* 20(1): 85–106	Data on investment banks providing M&A advice in the U.K. between 1992 and 2001	Diversified firms benefit from hub-and-spoke networks more than specialized firms
Chapter 5	Li, S.X. and T.J. Rowley. 2002. Inertia and evaluation mechanisms in interorganizational partner selection: Syndicate formation among U.S. investment banks. *Academy of Management Journal* 45(6): 1104–1120	Data on investment banks participating in the market for new offerings in the U.S. between 1994 and 1998	Strategies to build open or closed ties
Chapter 5	Shipilov, A.V. and S.X. Li. 2012. The missing link: The effect of customers on the formation of relationships among producers in the multiplex triads. *Organization Science* 23(2): 472–491	Data on investment banks participating in the market for new offerings in the U.S. between 1980 and 2001	Strategies to build open or closed ties

Chapter 6	Shipilov, A.V. 2005. Should you bank on your network? Relational and positional embeddedness in the making of financial capital. *Strategic Organization* 3(3): 279–309	Investment banks participating in the market for new securities in Canada between 1952 and 1990	Advantages of high status
Chapter 6	Godart, F., A. Shipilov, and K. Claes. Forthcoming. The impact of outward personnel mobility networks on organizational creativity. *Organization Science*	Data on the global fashion houses and the careers of fashion designers between 2000 and 2010	Advantages of high status
Chapter 6	Rao, H., H.R. Greve, and G.F. Davis. 2001. Fool's gold: Social proof in the initiation and abandonment of coverage by Wall Street analysts. *Administrative Science Quarterly* 46(3): 502–526	All firms listed in the National Issues Market of NASDAQ (U.S.) between 1987 and 1994	Advantages of high status
Chapter 8	Greve, H.R., H. Mitsuhashi, and J.A.C. Baum. 2013. Greener pastures: Outside options and strategic alliance withdrawal. *Organization Science* 24(1): 79–98	Data on shipping line operators originating from 37 nations. The data extend from 1988 through 2005	Firms terminate alliances when there are potential partners with higher complementarity

the simpler analytical tools presented throughout the chapters. We also summarize these simpler tools in Appendix Two.

Data

We downloaded information on alliances and joint ventures between firms from SDC Platinum Database owned by Thomson Reuters.[1] The data covered the period from 2008 to 2011 and is based on publicly available alliance or joint venture announcements. It is possible that this database doesn't cover all of the alliances between companies, so if your firm's alliance with a protagonist in the book (e.g. Sony, Samsung, Intel) is missing in our figures, don't worry, we have nothing against your firm and we did not drop it from our maps on purpose. All databases have limitations and should be considered as large samples of alliances from the universe of actual alliances which firms make. One recent paper compared different databases routinely used by alliance researchers and showed that the coverage in SDC Platinum did not have a systematic bias; the results based on SDC data are replicable using data from other databases.[2]

We constructed a global alliance network based on this data by building symmetric matrices in which rows and columns represented firms. An entry xij in this matrix represented an alliance between two firms i and j. In other words, firm i's list of direct partners can be identified by selecting non-zero cells j in the matrix. SDC identifies ultimate owners of the firms in the database. For example, an alliance between KEPCO and Westinghouse Electric will show up as an alliance between

---

[1] http://thomsonreuters.com/products_services/financial/financial_products/a-z/sdc/.

[2] Schilling, M. 2009. Understanding the alliance data. *Strategic Management Journal* 30(3): 233–260.

KEPCO and Toshiba on our network maps, because Toshiba owns Westinghouse Electric.

Software

We extracted first-, second- and third-degree networks for selected firms using the UCINET network analysis package.[3] To visualize the networks, we used NodeXL visualization software.[4] When networks were too large, especially when it came to visualizing the third degree (see the KEPCO third-degree network map in Chapter 6, for example), we input names of partners into the graphs by using image-editing software like Adobe's Photoshop.[5]

Network Advantage Measures

First Degree

For each firm i, the first-degree relationships can be captured by simply looking at the values in cells j in row i of the global alliance matrix. If the value is not equal to zero, then there is an alliance between a firm i and a partner j.

Second Degree

To identify whether firms had an integrated, hub-and-spoke or a hybrid alliance portfolio, we used the network constraint measure. In essence, this measure captures whether there are alliances between the firm's partners. Greater constraint means that the network is integrated, while smaller constraint means that the network is hub-and-spoke. Technical details on how this measure is calculated are available on page 55, equation 2.4 of Ron Burt's famous book *Structural Holes: The Social*

---

[3] https://sites.google.com/site/ucinetsoftware/home.
[4] http://nodexl.codeplex.com/.
[5] http://www.photoshop.com/.

Structure of Competition.[6] This measure was computed using UCINET software. There are several other measures available (effective size, efficiency, hierarchy), but we like constraint more because it takes into account both the number of partners in a firm's alliance portfolio and the presence (or absence) of alliances between them.

Third Degree

To calculate status for each firm, we used Bonacich's eigenvector centrality measure.[7] The idea behind this measure is that the centrality of a firm is determined by the centrality (i.e. number of partners) of the firms it is connected to. Imagine two firms A and B that have four partners each. If each partner of firm A has two partners of its own, but each partner of firm B has five partners of its own, then firm B is of higher status. This measure was also computed using UCINET software. This is a standard approach for calculating status in academic research on networks. Once we computed this measure for all firms in the global network of alliances, we identified the firms which had the highest eigenvector centrality scores (KEPCO had the highest).

---

[6] Burt, R. 1992. *Structural Holes: The Social Structure of Competition.* Cambridge, MA: Harvard University Press.

[7] Bonacich, P. 1972. Factoring and weighting approaches to status scores and clique identification. *Journal of Mathematical Sociology* 2: 113–120.

THE TOOLBOX

This appendix contains the following exercises:

1. The First-Degree Assessment Tool (introduced in Chapter 3)
2. The Second-Degree Assessment Tool (introduced in Chapter 5)
3. The Third-Degree Assessment Tool (introduced in Chapter 7)
4. The Build or Join Tool (introduced in Chapter 8)
5. The Alliance Portfolio Jigsaw Tool (introduced in Chapter 10)

The First-Degree Assessment Tool

Note: This tool is introduced in Chapter 3.

Task: Think about a specific strategic alliance which your firm currently has or is planning to have. Evaluate this specific partner in terms of the Four Dimensions of Fit.

My company name: _____

My partner name: _____

Step 1: Strategy Fit

- What are each partner's key objectives for this alliance?

My company	Partner company

- What are the key performance indicators for this alliance from the standpoint of both partners?

My company	Partner company

- Are the partners current competitors or are they likely to compete in the same product or geographic markets in the future? If so, which ones?

- How can this alliance help each partner achieve competitive advantage (by lowering costs, increasing product/service differentiation or both)?

My company	Partner company

- When will the partners exit the alliance? What are the terms of alliance termination?

Based on these answers, evaluate the **strategy fit** of this alliance using the following rating scale:

(1—no fit at all, 3—some fit, but not great, 5—great fit)

1 2 3 4 5

Step 2: Resource Fit
- What resources does each partner contribute to the relationship? Contributions can be knowledge, technology, financial, intellectual property, brand, market access, human capital and so on. Are they similar or different?

My company	Partner company

- How will the resources that each partner brings make the resources of the other partner more valuable?

My company	Partner company

- What return on the contributed resources does each partner plan to obtain? How will each partner evaluate this return?

My company	Partner company

- How will each partner's resource contributions change over time?

Time period	My company	Partner company
Current year		
Next year		

Based on these answers, evaluate the **resource fit** of this alliance using the following rating scale:

(1—no fit at all, 3—some fit, but not great, 5—great fit)

1 2 3 4 5

Step 3: Organization Fit

- What are the organizational structures of each firm (e.g. flat, hierarchical, matrix)? Are they similar or different?

My company	Partner company

- How quickly does each organization make decisions? How many layers of bureaucracy are involved in decision making?

My company	Partner company

- What is the ownership form of each partner? Are they similar or different?

My company	Partner company

- Have the partners collaborated in previous relationships? How successful were these relationships?

Based on these answers, evaluate the **organization fit** of this alliance using the following rating scale:

(1—no fit at all, 3—some fit, but not great, 5—great fit)

1 2 3 4 5

Step 4: Culture Fit

• What are the cultural values and belief systems of each partner? Are they similar or different?

My company	Partner company

• How does each partner handle conflict and uncertainty?

My company	Partner company

• What is each partner's attitude toward risk taking?

My company	Partner company

- How does each partner deal with new ideas?

My company	Partner company

- Are both partners looking for win–win solutions in alliances?

My company	Partner company

- Do both partners share the same national culture?

Based on these answers, evaluate the **culture fit** of this alliance using the following rating scale:

(1—no fit at all, 3—some fit, but not great, 5—great fit)

1   2   3   4   5

Step 5: Reflect on Results

- For an existing alliance:
  - Should this alliance be continued?

  - What dimensions of fit do you need to work on to improve this alliance?

- For a new alliance:
  - Should you form this alliance?

  - What additional information do you need? Where can you get this information?

Figure A.1: Alliance Fit Chart

Partner name	Strategy fit	Resource fit	Organization fit	Culture fit
Rating	1 to 5	1 to 5	1 to 5	1 to 5

The Second-Degree Assessment Tool

Note: This tool is introduced in Chapter 5.

Task: Evaluate whether your alliance portfolio is currently hub-and-spoke, integrated, or hybrid. Determine whether this configuration is optimal given your industry dynamism, your firm's range of products or services, and your firm's market power.

Step 1: Draw a Picture of Your Alliance Portfolio

If your firm has fewer than 13 partners, you can draw a full picture of your portfolio:

1. In the center of the space below draw a circle which represents your firm. Write your firm's name in the circle.
2. How many alliance partners does your firm have? Draw this number of circles around your firm's circle. Write each partner's name in one of the circles. Use lines to connect your firm's circle with your partners' circles.
3. Which of your partners have alliances or similar collaborations with each other? Use lines to connect the circles of those partners.

If your firm has more than 13 partners, you can draw a simplified picture of your portfolio:

1. In the space below, draw a circle to represent your firm and then add other circles around it to represent your alliance partners. Organize similar types of partners in groups by type of business. Also, group similar smaller partners together.
2. If some of your partners are collaborators with each other, use lines to draw connections between the circles for these partners; if not, keep the circles separated.

3. To make the picture more informative, next to each partner
   name indicate the key insights you gained from the First-
   Degree Assessment exercise. That is, write each partner's
   rating for the Four Dimensions of Fit—strategy, resource,
   culture, and organization fit—as well as the key benefits that
   your company gets from each partner (or group of partners,
   if applicable).

Step 2: Count and Analyze Open and Closed Ties

Make this table as big as you need it. When filling out the table, write the name of each partner *only once* in the left-hand column of the table under "Partner company." In the center column under "Partner's connections to other partners," list the names of all your partners that also have alliances with this partner. In the right-hand column, if that partner has no alliances with your other partners, put a check mark to label that partner as an open tie. After you complete this chart, it will be easy to make bar graphs like the ones shown in Figure 5.2 of Chapter 5.

Partner company	Partner's connections to other partners (list all partners)	Is the tie open?

Partner company	Partner's connections to other partners (list all partners)	Is the tie open?

This table also shows:

- how *many* partnerships there are among your partners;
- *which* of your partners is best connected to your other partners.

If you have a very big and complex alliance portfolio, use the example in Figure 5.2 of Chapter 5 to depict the number of open and closed ties in the table above.

If your firm is active in a number of very different industries, you may want to group your partners by industry and count the number of open and closed ties for each industry.

Step 3: Use the Configuration Alignment Tool (CAT)

1. To help you determine the most appropriate configuration for your alliance portfolio, answer these three questions:

    I   What is the level of dynamism facing your industry?

    1 = Low: there is little volatility in demand/supply, we can predict the direction of changes in the industry with reasonable accuracy, disruptive innovations are not common

    2 = Medium: there is some volatility in demand/supply, predicting the direction of changes in the industry is challenging but doable, disruptive innovations appear sometimes

    3 = High: there is huge volatility in demand/supply, we have a hard time predicting the direction of changes in the industry, disruptive innovations appear very often

    II   What is the range of your firm's product or service offering?

    1 = Narrow: we are specialized product/service providers and have a single (or very few) offerings

    2 = Mixed: neither narrow nor broad, about average in our industry

    3 = Broad: we have a wide range of products and services

    III   How much market power does your firm wield in the industry?

    1 = Low market power: small market share, few financial resources

    2 = Medium market power: average market share, average financial resources

    3 = High market power: highest market share in the industry or major financial resources

2. Summarize your firm's responses by circling your answers on the grid below:

Integrated	Hybrid	Hub-and-spoke
Industry dynamism		
1 = Low	2 = Medium	3 = High
Product (or service) range		
1 = Narrow	2 = Mixed	3 = Broad
Market power		
1 = Low	2 = Medium	3 = High

3. Interpretation of your answers:
   a. If most answers are to the left of the grid, then your portfolio needs to be integrated; in other words you benefit if your partners work together.
   b. If most answers are to the right of the grid, then your portfolio needs to be mostly hub-and-spoke. That is, you benefit from being the broker among disconnected partners.
   c. If most answers are at the center of the grid, then you need a hybrid portfolio. That is, you will benefit when some of your partners are connected and the others are not.

Step 4: Develop Portfolio Adjustment Plan

1. If you need to make your portfolio more "hub-and-spoke" by forming more open ties, think about these partnering opportunities. List the possibilities here.

   - Makers of complements—they produce products or services that make your own product or service more valuable.

   - Makers of substitutes—they make products or services that are different from yours, but address the same customer needs.

   - New industry entrants—firms that entered your industry within the past three years to which your current partners are not connected.

   - Your partners' direct competitors.

   - Your direct competitors.

2. If you need to make your portfolio more "integrated" by forming more closed ties, think about taking these partnering actions. List the possibilities.

   ■ Make referrals. Which two of your current partners could work together?

   ■ Seek referrals. Ask your current partner to introduce you to one of its partners.

   ■ Neutralize a broker. Is there a firm that acts as an intermediary between you and some other firm? You can neutralize this broker by establishing a direct relationship with that other firm.

   ■ Form a union. Can you and some firms in your industry gain economies of scale by working together?

Step 5: Reflect on the Results

- Does your portfolio structure match the optimal structure determined by the Configuration Alignment Tool?

- What new partnering opportunities did you discover? Which of these potential partners have the best strategy, resource, organization, and culture fit with your firm?

- What additional information do you need? Where can you get this information?

The Third-Degree Assessment Tool

Note: This tool is introduced in Chapter 7.

Task: Understand the status of your firm and develop strategies for enhancing your status.

Step 1: Identify High-Status Firms

1. In the space below, identify the Top 10 firms that you think are the most influential and respected in your industry. These could be direct competitors, customers, suppliers, or makers of complements (products that are used with yours).

Step 2: Position Your Firm

1. Ask yourself: Do you think your firm belongs in this list? Be honest.
2. Do you think that the outside observer (customer, supplier, or competitor) would agree with you?
3. If your firm belongs in the list of Top 10 firms in your industry, then it is probably a high-status partner. If it doesn't belong in this list, then it is a low-status partner.

Step 3: Enhance or Sustain Your Status

Let's assume that your firm has a consistent price/quality combination for your products and/or services. Given this assumption, think about these two questions:

- How can you sustain your position if you are a high-status firm?
- How can you increase your status if you are a low-status firm? Consider taking some of these actions:
  1. Partner with a high-status firm:
     - Which of the high-status firms are your partners?

     - If you don't yet have such high-status partners, what might you offer to them? Note: You can think about ways to increase your attractiveness to high-status partners by taking some of the actions below.

  2. Take a leadership role in industry events:
     - What industry events are your senior executives currently participating in?

     - Do your executives play a leadership role in these events? Is playing a leadership role in industry events a part of their job description?

- If your executives are not playing any role in any industry events now, which industry events could they participate in going forward?

- When was the last time your firm's cases were discussed at a major industry event?

- How and when should your firm approach the organizers of such events to increase your visibility there?

3. Become a spokesperson for a critical issue:
   - What is the critical issue that energizes your industry?

   - What has your firm done to bring forward new thinking on this issue?

- How much support would your executives get from your communications department in order to publicize to a broader audience your firm's message about or position on this critical issue?

4. Convene an event:
   - What is one industry event that doesn't exist yet, but that your firm could convene on an annual or bi-annual basis?

   - How does this event fit with the critical industry issue?

   - What key participants would you invite?

   - How would you communicate about this event and who else from your industry could participate in it?

5. Report small wins:
   - Do you have small wins to report from your relationships with existing alliance partners (especially if they are high-status partners)?

   - What media can you use to report these small wins? Joint blogs, joint press releases, an industry conference?

   - Which partners might be more open to publicizing these small wins themselves?

6. Champion thought leadership:
   - What does your firm know that you can share with the world? Knowledge about products and services, industry trends, new markets?

- What alliance management experience do you have?

- Who would be interested in writing about what you have done (e.g. journalists, business school professors)?

- How can you communicate to the world what you know?

Step 4: Reflection

- What three key actions will you take within the next three months to enhance your firm's status?

The Build or Join Tool

Note: This tool is introduced in Chapter 8.

Task: Understand whether you should build your own alliance portfolio or join the alliance network of another firm.

Step 1: Assess the Autonomy and Attractiveness of Your Firm

Answer the following questions in order to assess how autonomous your firm is in its industry and how attractive it is to others.

Autonomy

- Uniqueness
  - Do you have few or no close competitors for your product or service? Many competitors indicate low uniqueness and autonomy.

  - When you launch a new product, does it take a long time for a competing product to be introduced? A short time period indicates low uniqueness and autonomy.

  - If you do not have a close competitor, do significant barriers exist that prevent others from imitating your product or service? High barriers indicate high autonomy.

If you answer, "yes" to most or all of these questions, then your firm has "high" uniqueness and autonomy.

- Brokerage

  - Is your position in the industry one that has an interface with the customer and collects information on the customer? If yes, this is an indication of high autonomy.

  - Is your position in the industry one that integrates components, technologies, activities, or services? If yes, this is an indication of your autonomy.

If you answer, "yes" to one or both of these questions, then your firm performs a brokerage function and has "high" autonomy.

Attraction

- High status
  - Is your firm high status? Use the tool in Chapter 7. Pay special attention to the network status, because alliance partners will be concerned about your quality as a collaboration partner. High status translates into high attraction.

- Clear vision
  - Can you articulate a vision for the alliance portfolio, with clearly explained roles for each member and an explanation for how they contribute value and will benefit from their contribution? The presence of clear vision indicates high attraction.

If you answer, "yes" to one or both of these questions, then your firm has "high" attractiveness.

- Do the answers above indicate that your autonomy and attraction are, overall, high or low compared with other firms in the industry? Be specific and realistic.

Step 2: Find Your Position in the Matrix

		Autonomy	
		Low	High
Attractiveness	Low	#1—Improve autonomy or attractiveness	#2—Build attractiveness
	High	#3—Join an alliance network	#4—Build an alliance portfolio

Identify the optimal strategy for your firm by positioning it in the matrix based on your answers about your firm's autonomy and attraction.

Step 3: Reflect on Possible Actions

Write an action plan that fits your position in the matrix.

- If you find yourself in position #1, how can you improve your autonomy or attractiveness?

- If you find yourself in position #2, how can you build attractiveness?

- If you find yourself in position #3, which alliance network can you join?

- If you find yourself in position #4, how will you build your alliance portfolio?

The Alliance Portfolio Jigsaw Tool

Note: This tool is introduced in Chapter 10.

Task: Identify areas where you can create value by combining resources from multiple partners.

Step 1: Picture Overlapping Alliances

- Pick three or four key alliance partners you have now.
- Draw the corresponding number of overlapping circles and write each partner's name in a circle.
- Define the current objectives you have with each partner and the resources each partner currently has. Jot these in each partner's circle. Keep the category of partner resources intentionally broad and include intangible resources, tangible resources, and social resources (in other words, the partner's ties to others).

Step 2: Conceptualize Opportunities That Combine Partner Resources

- Take each pair of partners (overlapping circles) and think about projects or initiatives that you could start if you combined resources from each one of them.
- Repeat this exercise with different partner configurations in order to identify opportunities for greater network advantage in each configuration.

Step 3: Determine How to Proceed with Ideas

- Do you want to realize these opportunities as a part of a hub-and-spoke or an integrated portfolio? This decision will depend on your firm's optimal portfolio configuration (discussed in Chapter 5).
  - Integrated portfolio: If your firm is in a stable industry, has low market power, or is a specialist with narrow

product/service range, then you are better off bringing partners together for initiatives.

- Hub-and-spoke portfolio: If your firm competes in a more dynamic industry, has higher market power, or has a broad product range, then you should try keeping these partners separate and realize the network advantage by continuing to play a hub role between them.

Step 4: Apply the Concept More Broadly

- Do the same exercise with the list of potential partners you generated in Chapter 5 (Five Ways to Build Open Ties and Four Ways to Build Closed Ties).
  - Pick some makers of complementary products, makers of substitutes, new industry entrants, or your competitors. Ask yourself whether you could create new and valuable combinations by collaborating with them as well as with your existing partners.
  - You can do this by adding additional circles to your Jigsaw, indicating in them what resources you could get from these potential partners, and thinking through new combinations that you could create with them.
- Use this tool to think about opportunities for realizing third-degree network advantage.
  - Which firms among the potential partners you identified above have high status? The exercise in Chapter 7 (Third-Degree Assessment Tool) could help you with this step.
  - If you see valuable combinations that could be created between your existing partners and a potential high-status partner, make sure the high-status partner knows about them. This can be done without revealing which of your partners are the sources of these resources.

Template for the Alliance Portfolio Jigsaw with three partners

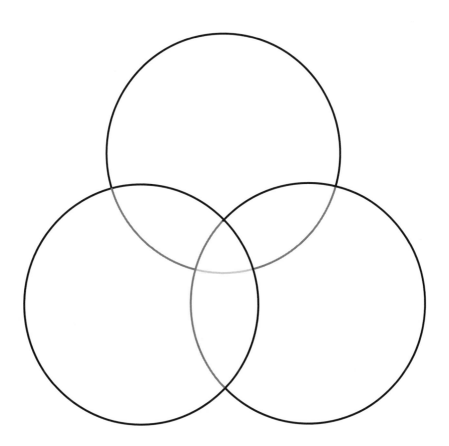

APPENDIX THREE

DIRECTORY OF COMPANY NAMES

For ease of reading, we refer to the companies discussed in the book by their commonly known names or shortened versions of these common names. This appendix contains a listing of common names used along with the full corporate entity names. This listing is sorted alphabetically by common name.

Common name	Full corporate entity name
AB InBev	Anheuser-Busch InBev
AMD	Advanced Micro Devices
BioInvent	BioInvent International
Biocon	Biocon Limited
BMG	Bertelsmann Music Group
BMI	British Midland International
DreamWorks	DreamWorks Animation SKG
DuPont	E.I. DuPont de Nemours & Co.
Genentech	Genetic Engineering Technology
GM	General Motors
Hennessy	Jas Hennessy & Co.
Intel	Intel Corporation
LVMH	Louis Vuitton Moët Hennessy
MAAF	MAAF Assurances
MACIF	MACIF Fiche

Common name	Full corporate entity name
MAIF	Mutuelle Assurance Instituteur France
NXP	NXP Semiconductors
Philips Electronics (Philips)	Koninklijke Philips Electronics N.V. ADS
Pixar	Pixar Animation Studios
Rabobank	Rabobank Groep N.V.
Samsung	Samsung Electronics
Sberbank	Sberbank of Russia
Sierra On-line	Sierra Entertainment
Syngene	Syngene International
Toronto Maple Leafs	Toronto Maple Leaf Hockey Club
Ubisoft	Ubisoft Entertainment

Glossary

alliance: an enduring and formalized collaborative relationship between two firms that involves significant exchange of information and resources. Alliances include strategic alliances and joint ventures as well as any enduring buyer–supplier, joint manufacturing, R&D, or licensing agreements between firms.

alliance network: the system of alliances that interconnects all firms within an industry.

alliance partners: two firms connected through a collaborative alliance relationship.

alliance portfolio: a collective term referring to a firm's "thick-line" relationship with its group of alliance partners.

alliance portfolio-building style: a firm's consistent pattern of alliance formation over time.

autonomy: how independent a firm is to make its own decisions on how to configure exchange flows in the industry.

compatible partners: firms that trust each other and have similar skills and routines that make it easy to work together.

complementary partners: firms that bring different skills and knowledge which they combine in order to achieve their objective.

cultural fit: the extent to which firms have similar cultures so that they can understand, appreciate, and work within each other's values and beliefs.

ecosystem: a group of organizations that have some common goal.

first-degree network advantage: benefits which come from a firm's ability to combine its resources and capabilities with the resources and capabilities of each individual alliance partner.

first-degree perspective: seeing only the individual alliance partnerships.

hub-and-spoke: an alliance portfolio in which one firm operates at the center (the hub) and is connected like spokes in a wheel to partners that are mostly not connected to each other.

hybrid: a combination of integrated and hub-and-spoke, this is an alliance portfolio where a firm has some connected and some unconnected partners.

integrated: refers to an alliance portfolio in which a firm is connected to partners that are also mostly connected to each other.

network advantage: gaining more information, cooperation, and power benefits from alliances and the firm's position in the industry's alliance network as compared to competitors.

open and closed ties: open ties are the relationships with partners that are not connected to other partners of the firm. Closed ties are the relationships with partners that are connected to other partners of the firm.

organizational fit: the extent to which partners have compatible organizational structures, i.e. they have formal command and control mechanisms that are not different to the point that the companies cannot coordinate their decision making.

resource fit: the extent of complementarity between the resources which the partners bring to the table.

second-degree network advantage: the unique ability to get timely access to information, secure cooperation, and gain power by using the connections among a firm's alliance partners. The extent to which a firm's partners have alliances with one another determines the power, cooperation, and types of information flowing across the network.

second-degree perspective: looking at an organization's whole portfolio of alliances including alliances between partners.

status: the perceived influence and leadership a firm has in its industry.

strategy fit: the extent to which partners have complementary strategies.

third-degree network advantage: the ability to gain increased information, cooperation, and power benefits by having high status in the alliance network or by creating alliances with high-status partners.

third-degree perspective: seeing the network of ties connecting all firms in an industry.

Index